This book is due on the last date stamped below.
Failure to return books on the date due may result
in assessment of overdue fees.

FINES	.50 per day	

Karma

JOHANNES BRONKHORST

Dimensions of Asian Spirituality

UNIVERSITY OF HAWAI'I PRESS

Honolulu

DIMENSIONS OF ASIAN SPIRITUALITY
Henry Rosemont, Jr., General Editor

This series makes available short but comprehensive works on specific Asian philosophical and religious schools of thought, works focused on a specific region, and works devoted to the full articulations of a concept central to one or more of Asia's spiritual traditions. Series volumes are written by distinguished scholars in the field who not only present their subject matter in historical context for the nonspecialist reader, but also express their own views of the contemporary spiritual relevance of their subject matter for global citizens of the twenty-first century.

Library of Congress Cataloging-in-Publication Data
Bronkhorst, Johannes.
Karma / Johannes Bronkhorst.
p.   cm.—(Dimensions of Asian spirituality)
Includes bibliographical references and index.
ISBN 978-0-8248-3570-5 (hardcover : alk. paper)—ISBN 978-0-8248-3591-0 (pbk. : alk. paper)
1. Karma.   I. Title.   II. Series: Dimensions of Asian spirituality.
BL2015.K3B76 2011
202'.20954—dc22

2011005311

Designed by Rich Hendel

Printed by Sheridan Books, Inc.

Contents

Special Topics

Editor's Preface

ABOUT THIS SERIES

The University of Hawai'i Press has long been noted for its scholarly publications in, and commitment to, the field of Asian studies. This series, Dimensions of Asian Spirituality, is in keeping with that commitment. It is a most appropriate time for such a series to appear. A number of the world's religions—major and minor—originated in Asia, continue to influence significantly the lives of a third of the world's peoples, and should now be seen as global in scope, reach, and impact, with rich and varied resources for every citizen of the twenty-first century to explore.

Religion is at the heart of every culture. To be sure, the members of every culture have also been influenced by climate, geology, and by the consequent patterns of economic activity they have developed for the production and distribution of goods. Only a minimal knowledge of physical geography is necessary to understand why African sculptors largely employed wood as their medium while their Italian Renaissance equivalents worked with marble. But while necessary for understanding cultures—not least our own—matters of geography and economics will not be sufficient: marble is also found in China, yet the Chinese sculptor carved a bodhisattva, not a pietà, from his block.

In the same way, a mosque, synagogue, cathedral, stupa, and pagoda may be equally beautiful, but they are beautiful in different ways, and the differences cannot be accounted for merely on the basis of the materials used in their construction. Their beauty, their ability to inspire awe and to invite contemplation, rests largely on the religious view of the world—and the place of human beings in that world—that is expressed in their architecture. The spiritual dimensions of a culture are reflected significantly not only in art and architecture, but in music, myths, poetry, rituals, customs, and patterns of social behavior as well. Therefore it follows that if we wish to understand why and how members of other cultures live as they do, we must understand the religious beliefs and practices to which they adhere.

In the first instance, such understanding of the "other" leads to tolerance, which is surely a good thing. Much of the pain and suffering in the world today is attributable to intolerance, a fear and hatred of those who look, think, and act differently. But as technological changes in communication, production, and transportation shrink the world, more and more people must confront the fact of human diversity in multiply diverse forms—both between and within nations—and hence there is a growing need to go beyond mere tolerance of difference to an appreciation and celebration of it. Tolerance alone cannot contribute substantively to making the world a better—and sustainable—place for human beings to live, the evils attendant on intolerance notwithstanding and not to be diminished. But in an important sense, mere tolerance is easy because passive: I can fully respect your right to believe and worship as you wish, associate with whomever, and say what you will, simply by ignoring you; you assuredly have a right to speak, but not to make me listen.

Yet for most of us who live in economically developed societies, or are among the affluent in developing nations, tolerance is not enough. Ignoring the poverty, disease, and gross inequalities that afflict fully a third of the human race will only exacerbate, not alleviate, the conditions responsible for the misery that generates the violence becoming ever more commonplace throughout the world today. That violence will cease only when the more fortunate among the peoples of the world become active, take up the plight of the less fortunate, and resolve to create and maintain a more just world, a resolve that requires a full appreciation of the co-humanity of everyone, significant differences in religious beliefs and practices notwithstanding.

Such appreciation should not, of course, oblige everyone to endorse all of the beliefs and practices within their own faith. A growing number of Catholics, for instance, support changes in church practice: a married clergy, the ordination of women, recognition of rights for gays and lesbians, and full reproductive rights for women. Yet they remain Catholics, believing that the tenets of their faith have the conceptual resources to bring about and justify these changes. In the same way, we can also believe—as a number of Muslim women do—that the *Quran* and other Islamic theological writings contain the conceptual resources to overcome the inferior status of women in some Muslim countries. And indeed we can believe that every spiritual tradition has within it the resources to counter older practices inimical to the full flourishing of all the faithful—and of the faithful of other traditions as well.

Another reason to go beyond mere tolerance to appreciation and celebration of the many and varied forms of spiritual expression is virtually a truism: the more we look through a window on another culture's beliefs and practices, the more it becomes a mirror of our own (even for those who follow no religious tradition). We must look carefully and charitably, however, else the reflections become distorted. When studying other religions, most people are inclined to focus on cosmological and ontological questions, asking, What do these people believe about how the world came to be, is, and where is it heading? Do they believe in ghosts? Immortal souls? A creator god?

Answering these and related metaphysical questions is of course necessary for understanding and appreciating the specific forms and content of the art, music, architecture, rituals, and traditions inspired by the specific religion under study. But the sensitive—and sensible—student will bracket the further question of whether the metaphysical pronouncements are literally true; we must attend carefully to the metaphysics (and theologies) of the religions we study, but questions of their literal truth should be set aside to concentrate on a different question: how could a thoughtful, thoroughly decent human being subscribe to and follow these beliefs and attendant practices?

Studied in this light, we may come to see and appreciate how each religious tradition provides a coherent account of a world not fully amenable to human manipulation, nor perhaps even to full human understanding. The metaphysical pronouncements of the world's religions of course differ measurably from faith to faith, and each has had a significant influence on the physical expressions of the respective faith in synagogues, stupas, mosques, pagodas, and cathedrals. Despite these differences between the buildings, however, the careful and sensitive observer can see the spiritual dimensions of human life that these sacred structures share and express, and in the same way we can come to see and appreciate the common spiritual dimensions of each religion's differing metaphysics and theology: while the several traditions give different answers to the question of the meaning *of* life, they provide a multiplicity of guidelines and spiritual disciplines to enable everyone to find meaning *in* life, in this world. By plumbing the spiritual depths of other religious traditions, then, we may come to more deeply explore the spiritual resources of our own and at the same time diminish the otherness of the other and create a more peaceable and just world, in which everyone can find meaning in their all-too-human lives.

ABOUT THIS BOOK

Against this background we may place the present volume in the Dimensions of Asian Spirituality series, *Karma,* by Johannes Bronkhorst. Throughout most of its history karma has been a basic but highly contested concept among and between the several schools of religious and philosophical thought in South Asia, and Johannes Bronkhorst illuminates many of their differences by engagingly describing how each of them, especially Jainism, Buddhism, and the varied strands of Brahmanism, confront the problems attendant on taking seriously the dual senses of karma he takes as central to the term within its cultural and historical context(s).

These two meanings are *rebirth* and *retribution*. The two notions are, as Bronkhorst well notes, at least semi-independent of each other: On the one hand, one might be reborn endlessly just because that is the way things are, just as coal is black. On the other hand, one may equally believe that our world is just, that the goodwill be rewarded and evildoers punished in their present lives. But with respect to this latter position, there is a not inconsequential amount of evidence to suggest otherwise: many good people die young and/or undergo much misery in their lives, while many reprobates live out their full three score and ten in wealth and good health despite their misdeeds.

Bronkhorst takes up each of these senses of karma in some depth before turning to analyses of how they were developed and integrated by the several schools of Indian thought, working largely in the tra-

dition of close textual readings. First, and importantly, he emphasizes that in understanding karma as rebirth we must also understand that the overall connotation of the term is not a positive one.
At first blush it might seem that a doctrine of endless rebirths would
take away most of the dread accompanying thoughts of our eventual
demise and hence be truly a gospel: if, in the end, there is no end at
which we simply become worm food but go on to lead human lives
again, that seems to be good news indeed! Upon reflection, however,
the news might not be so good. If there is a sense in which each of our
lives may be said to be a story—an ongoing narrative—then someday
it must come to an end, just as it had a beginning and is now developing. While the idea of dying an hour from now is frightening, it is
perhaps less so than the idea of living forever, either in our current or
another human form. What meaning could such an endless string of
existences possibly have for anyone?

In this way we might come to sympathize with those thinkers
who sought a way to break the retributive dimension of karma and
thereby equally break the cycle of death and rebirth, as the two major
meanings of the concept came to be intertwined. Bronkhorst ably describes the different means developed by Jains, Buddhists, and Brah-
manists of one school or another to effect the breakage and along
the way directly addresses a number of other puzzles attendant on
coming to terms with the notions of rebirth and retribution, such as
what drives the retributive factor, especially when the idea of a good
deed is as highly contested as any other in the philosophical dia-
logues and disputations. As Bronkhorst himself analyzes it, we seem
to need a "karmic accountant" of some kind to decide on both which
deeds are good and which bad, and how, when, and where to allocate
the appropriate rewards and punishments attendant on those deeds.
Whence such an accountant, and why?

There is much more of significance in this little book, ranging
from an account of Jain "immobility asceticism" to a fresh analysis of
the concept of the self *(an/atman)* in Buddhism. And the reader will
learn much more that doctrinally distinguishes many of the major
schools of Brahmanism from each other in ways linked to the concept of karma.

In sum, the breadth and depth of Bronkhorst's account of karma makes the ideas associated with it come alive in the lives of South Asians of the past and thereby for everyone in the present, making it a most appropriate addition to the Dimensions of Asian Spirituality series.

HENRY ROSEMONT, JR.

Preface

This book deals with a belief that was current in a culture different from the one of its intended readers. It is not about karma in modern Western culture, but about karma in ancient and classical Indian culture. This book is therefore about aspects of a different culture, and I, as author, have the task of presenting a bridge between these two cultures. This is a serious responsibility, for in constructing such a bridge much can go wrong. Two extreme positions in particular must be avoided. According to one of these two, the gap between different cultures is unbridgeable. Clearly, this extreme is rejected by the very fact of trying to build such a bridge. The other extreme would be to underestimate the width of the gap or even to deny that there is one. This extreme is harder to avoid. The very act of trying to explain beliefs and concepts of one culture to readers who belong to another one has to part from the assumption that such an understanding across cultural boundaries is possible. This assumption easily gives rise to the idea that all human beings are basically the same, that for an understanding of aspects of another culture it is sufficient to draw upon our shared humanity. This idea is not altogether wrong: we are no doubt better prepared to study another *human* culture than, say, a culture of Martians (yet to be discovered). But simply feeling our way into isolated aspects of other (human) cultures is not enough. It is rarely possible to isolate aspects from the culture to which they belong without damaging them, without turning them into caricatures of what they are in their proper context.

The problem here raised is well-known to translators, who translate texts from one language (and culture) into another. The aim of many translations into English is to provide fluent versions of the foreign text, to "domesticate" it to the extent possible, with the result that readers are least aware of the fact that they are reading something foreign. Critics are familiar with the dangers of such translations, which risk, for example, imposing altogether different values and prejudices, the values and prejudices of English language readers, on a text.

The attempt to present beliefs and concepts from ancient and classical India to modern Western readers is confronted with similar problems. Beliefs and concepts have their place in certain cultural contexts. Taking them out of those contexts is more than likely to disfigure them. Without their proper context they will inevitably be interpreted in terms of the culture of the modern Western reader and may, in the end, come to mean something altogether different from what they meant in their original context.

In order to avoid all these pitfalls, modern interpreters have to observe some important rules. To begin with, they must be and remain aware of the sources that provide us with all the knowledge we have about the beliefs and concepts concerned. In the case of karma, these sources are almost exclusively textual. Texts can be translated and interpreted. The dangers connected with translating texts have been hinted at above; they are minor in comparison with those that arise when trying to interpret the beliefs and concepts these texts give expression to.

The first rule to be observed is that the interpreter stay close to the original texts and abstain to the extent possible from offering interpretations that are not themselves supported by textual evidence. Without explicit textual support such interpretations will more likely than not give expression to the interpreter's (modern Western) values and prejudices. However, and this takes us to the second rule, research can sometimes identify wider complexes of ideas in which the beliefs and concepts studied have their place. If, and only if, such wider complexes have been reliably identified, something like a contextual understanding becomes a possibility.

It is my purpose in the following pages to offer a contextual understanding of the beliefs and concepts related to karma where and to the extent that I am able do so. I can often do so, but not always. Beliefs and concepts that do not obviously fit into larger complexes of ideas will therefore be presented with a minimum of interpretation from my side. In such cases the best I can do is to allow the texts to speak for themselves (to the extent that is possible). Too much "help" in such cases, even from a modern Western or modern Indian "specialist," is likely to do more harm than good. Indeed, one modern scholar rightly warned against "modern speculative *opinions* about karma."

The presentation of karma in the following pages is guided by the preceding reflections. Where and to the extent that karma is part of a wider complex of ideas, the discussion will include that wider complex. Direct citation of source texts in such cases is avoided. The presentation of material that has not so far been shown to be part of a wider complex of ideas will rely more heavily on direct citations (in English translation) from source texts.

Introduction

Webster's Third New International Dictionary of the English Language has the following to say about karma:

> 1. the force generated by a person's actions that is held in Hinduism and Buddhism to be the motive power for the round of rebirths and deaths endured by him until he has achieved spiritual liberation and freed himself from the effects of such force;
>
> 2. the sum total of the ethical consequences of a person's good or bad actions comprising thoughts, words, and deeds that is held in Hinduism and Buddhism to determine his specific destiny in his next existence;
>
> 3. a subtle form of matter held in Jainism to develop in the soul and vitiate its purity, to lengthen the course of individual transmigration, and to postpone the possibility of final salvation.

This dictionary entry, inevitably, concerns the word *karma* as it is used in the English language. By and large this corresponds to the way—more precisely: one of the ways—in which the word is used in Sanskrit and other Indian languages.

In Sanskrit, the word can be used in many other ways as well. Apte's *Practical Sanskrit-English Dictionary,* for example, gives the following fifteen meanings: (1) Action, works, deed. (2) Execution, performance. (3) Business, office, duty. (4) A religious rite. (5) A specific action, moral duty. (6a) Performance of religious rites as opposed to speculative religion or knowledge of Brahman. (6b) Labour, work. (7) Product, result. (8) A natural or active property (as support of the earth). (9) Fate, the certain consequence of acts done in a former life. (10) (In grammar) The object of an action. (11) (In philosophy) Motion considered as one of the seven categories of things. (12) Organ of sense. (13) Organ of action. (14) (In Astronomy) The tenth lunar mansion. (15) Practice, training.

This multiplicity of meanings is hardly exceptional in Sanskrit, where many words have a sometimes impressive number of unrelated or barely related meanings. In the case of *karma,* however, it has led some scholars to the mistaken assumption that the *karma* that is connected with the belief in rebirth (Apte's no. 9) is historically a development out of *karma* in the sense of "religious rite" (Apte's no. 4). In reality the two are quite independent of each other and originated in altogether different milieus.

As in Webster's dictionary entry, then, the Indian word *karma* can be used in connection with the belief in rebirth. This is the use of the word that interests us in this book. In order to make clear that two different notions are involved, it will be useful to speak of "rebirth and karmic retribution," using the adjective *karmic,* which, by the way, is not present in Webster's dictionary (but has found a place in the *Merriam-Webster Online Dictionary*). The belief in rebirth in one form or another is widespread in religions around the world, but in most of them karmic retribution plays no, or no important role. Belief in rebirth can therefore very well exist without the notion of karmic retribution. This is an important point, for scholarly research into the origin of karmic retribution in India has sometimes mistakenly drawn conclusions from the observation that the belief in rebirth is (weakly) present in the oldest surviving literature of India, the Veda (see the boxed text titled "The Veda" in Chapter 3). Indeed, the prior (but incorrect) conviction that the origin of karmic retribution must be looked for in the Veda has led certain scholars to postulate, without supporting evidence, that this notion must be related to the religious rites, also sometimes called *karma,* that are the central concern of Vedic literature.

It is clear from Webster's dictionary entry that karma is something that concerns individuals: a person will be reborn in accordance with his or her actions. This is indeed the kind of karma that is most often written and thought about in the surviving literature of India; we will call it *orthodox karma.* It is this orthodox karma that will be discussed in the first part of this book. The notion will be presented here in its historical development, a development that concerns the major religions of ancient and classical India, most notably Jainism, Buddhism, and Brahmanism, and involved intensive interaction between these and other religious currents. The presentation will require a certain amount of jumping forward and backward between these movements, and also some jumping forward and backward in time, but I will try to reduce this to a minimum.

Once the historical presentation is in place, the remainder of the first part will discuss some of the ways in which different currents of thought tried to come to terms with this belief: how does karma work, and why? It will become clear that karma came to exert a profound influence on Indian philosophy in several ways.

The orthodox karma of authors and scholars did not always coincide with more popular notions related to but yet different from this literary and philosophical concept. To do justice to these alternative notions, the second part of this book will deal with *variants of karma*. These include the belief in the possibility of transfer of merit and in devotion to God as a means to circumvent karmic retribution.

The concluding reflections will briefly consider some developments outside the Indian subcontinent, and I will then propose some thoughts regarding how to make sense of the belief in rebirth and karmic retribution.

PART I

ORTHODOX KARMA

CHAPTER 1

Origins and Religious Use

Vedic literature is not the place to look for the origins of the belief in karmic retribution (see below). Unfortunately there is no other literature to help us in this respect. The notion of karmic retribution pops up, so to say, in the literature of a region distinct from the homeland of Vedic literature: the earliest literature of Jainism and Buddhism. And it does not present itself, in that other literature, as a new notion, but as an old one, one that had become oppressive.

The belief that death is not the end, that there will be new lives afterward, perhaps in this same world, perhaps in decidedly more agreeable circumstances, should not necessarily be a source of pessimism. The further belief that one can influence the quality of one's future lives by what one does in the present might rather give rise to optimism. It is likely that many of those who believed in rebirth and karmic retribution were indeed attracted by the prospect of a better life afterwards and treated this belief as a source of hope. This attitude does not, however, find expression in the earliest surviving literature. The surviving literature usually takes an altogether different position. It deals with continued existence in future lives as a source of distress, as an endless repetition of suffering and unhappiness. The concern of those whose ideas find expression in that literature was not to assure an agreeable rebirth, but rather to put an end to rebirths altogether. Their aim was liberation from the endless cycle of rebirths. This much they agreed upon. They did not all agree on the way in which such a liberation can be attained.

There is, then, very little that can be said about the origin of the belief in rebirth and karmic retribution in India. By the time this belief manifests itself in the surviving literature, it is well established. Our literary sources present us not with the origin of this belief, but with ways to deal with its consequences. Liberation from rebirth and karmic retribution is the aim. Note that this is primarily a negative aim. The aim is not, or not primarily, a state of bliss or well-being in or after this life, but rather the definitive and irreversible termination of the sequence of lives one is otherwise condemned to live.

The particular context in which our early textual sources deal with the belief in rebirth and karmic retribution, and the reason why they do so, are to be kept in mind. As stated above, these sources are particularly interested in liberation from the endless cycle of rebirths. This, however, is a goal that does not fit in easily with the belief. Belief in rebirth and karmic retribution implies, primarily, that one will reap the rewards of the seeds one sows in this life, normally in a next life. Good deeds will give rise to agreeable forms of rebirth, bad deeds to disagreeable ones. Virtue is rewarded; vice is punished. This belief has an undeniable moral aspect: it implies that the universe has an in-built moral dimension. This is, of course, fine, or even reassuring, for those who wish to live an upright yet agreeable life and hope to continue doing so in a future existence but poses a problem for those who are fed up with it. For these last there is no obvious way out. Living a virtuous life is no solution; its consequence will be a more agreeable life, a life in which more of one's desires are fulfilled and therefore a life in which it will be even harder to separate oneself from its temptations. And a life of vice will be responsible for a future existence of misery and reduced mental capacities, which exclude the very possibility of intelligent action.

These reflections will make clear that a discussion of karma— that is, of the belief in rebirth and karmic retribution—cannot be limited to an exposition of this belief in its various manifestations. It is true that the belief has taken different shapes during its known history in the Indian subcontinent of some two and a half millennia. It is also true that there were different evaluations of what are good and what are bad deeds, depending on what particular religious current one belonged to. However, these issues cannot be discussed without taking into consideration the question that our textual

sources very frequently discuss along with them, the question as to
how individuals can free themselves from the karmic consequences
of their deeds. We will see that this question is not only inseparable
from the belief in rebirth and karmic retribution, it also has an effect on the shape this belief takes in different religious movements.
A historical presentation of a number of early religious movements
in northern India will make this clear. It is with such a presentation
that we therefore begin.

God and Gods in Indian Religions

In studying the indigenous religious history of South Asia, it
is important to keep in mind that we are faced with a variety
of religious movements that do not always have much in common with each other. One feature, however, applies to many
of them: religion in the Indian situation is not always identical with the worship of one or more gods. Notions like "belief" and "faith"—so common in the Abrahamic religions—are
only rarely applicable in the Indian situation, and where they
are, they cover something different altogether. The existence
of gods is not denied in Buddhism, Jainism, and Brahmanism,
but—at any rate during the early period—they are not central
to the religious efforts of the followers of these religions. These
religions accept the existence of gods and of many other invis-
ible, supernatural beings, but all these beings play a relatively
marginal role even in the minds of the most religiously moti-
vated people.

Brahmanical priestly speculation had a tendency to be impersonal (the gods in late-Vedic literature are a mere shadow of
the temperamental beings whose praise was sung in early Vedic hymns), and it is not therefore surprising that Brahmanical
speculation came to concern itself with an impersonal highest entity, Brahma, that did little beyond encompassing the
universe. Knowledge of this impersonal entity became highly
prized, as was the realization that one's inner self is identical with it. Beside this impersonal Brahma (the word is here
used in the neuter gender), there was also a personal god called

Brahma (used in the masculine), often thought of as the creator god. However, this god inspired no one to worship him.

Subsequent centuries saw the rise to prominence within the Brahmanical tradition of two gods in particular, Shiva and Vishnu. Worshipers tended to look upon one or the other as the supreme God (the use of a capital *G* now seems appropriate), so much so that most Hindus would look upon themselves as followers of one or the other. Both these Gods are surrounded by elaborate mythologies, which provide them with wives, enemies, and much else. The mythology of Vishnu is of particular interest in that it provides him with a number of incarnations *(avatara):* Vishnu was (and is) believed to have been born on earth in the form of a number of quasi-historical figures in order to restore order. The most famous of these *avataras* are Rama and Krishna. Rama is the hero of the Sanskrit epic called *Ramayana;* Krishna figures prominently in the other Sanskrit epic, the *Mahabharata,* and in other texts. Both Rama and Krishna became the object of personal devotion and continue to play a central role in *bhakti* (see below).

Occasionally the three gods Brahma, Vishnu, and Shiva are looked upon as constituting a trinity *(trimurti),* responsible for the creation, preservation, and destruction of the world respectively. Unlike Vishnu and Shiva, the creator god Brahma did not become the object of separate worship.

CHAPTER 2

Karma in and after
Greater Magadha

The region east of the Vedic homeland, that is, east of the confluence of the Ganges and the Jumna, in the eastern Ganges plane, may conveniently be called Greater Magadha. It saw the appearance of a number of religious currents during the centuries around the middle of the first millennium B.C.E. We will consider—after some introductory remarks about Greater Magadha—Jainism, Ajivikism, those who saw in knowledge of the self the key to the highest goal, and Buddhism.

Magadha was the name of a kingdom in the eastern Ganges valley. In the fourth century B.C.E. it became the center of an empire that at its height unified most of the Indian subcontinent, but Magadha and its surrounding regions—jointly to be referred to as Greater Magadha—was characterized by its own culture even before the creation of this empire and for some time after its collapse. It was in this area that urbanization took off again from approximately 500 B.C.E. onward (after the disappearance of the so-called Indus civilization more than a thousand years earlier).

The culture of Greater Magadha was in many respects different from Vedic culture, whose heartland was situated to its west. The two cultures could not but come in close contact, especially when the rulers of Magadha expanded their kingdom and included the Vedic heartland and much else into their empire (which reached its greatest extent under the Maurya emperor Ashoka). The resulting confrontation and sometimes assimilation of the two cultures constitutes the background against which much of the subsequent history of Indian culture has to be understood.

One of the most distinctive features of the culture of Greater Magadha was the belief in rebirth and karmic retribution. This explains why the religious movements that were based on this belief originated here. The best known of these religious movements are Jainism, Buddhism, and Ajivikism. The way in which this belief came to be adopted in Brahmanism, in spite of resistance that took many centuries to dissipate, will be explained in a later chapter. Note here that this belief came to be thought of in the Brahmanical tradition (and in modern scholarship until recently) as an inherent and inseparable part of it.

The cyclic vision of time—in which creations and destructions of the universe succeed each other in a beginningless and endless sequence—is another notion that originally belonged to Greater Magadha, only to be subsequently adopted and claimed as its own by Brahmanism. This vision is to be distinguished from the belief in a beginningless and endless sequence of births and deaths of sentient beings, but the parallelism between the two is easy to see.

Funerary practices, too, opposed the culture of Greater Magadha to Vedic culture. The inhabitants of Greater Magadha built round funerary tombs for their dead; it is possible that dead bodies were placed in those tombs, without prior incineration, but this is not certain. The custom survives in the stupas of the Buddhists and Jainas, and in the so-called *samadhi*s (funerary constructions) built for certain Hindu saints until today. Brahmanism absorbed in due time the belief in rebirth and karmic retribution (see below) but never accepted the funerary practices of its eastern neighbors, except in the exceptional case of certain Hindu saints.

There are good reasons to assume that Ayurveda, the classical form of Indian medicine, had its roots in the culture of Greater Magadha. Unlike the Vedic medical tradition, which heavily relied on sorcery, spells, and amulets, the medical tradition prevalent in Greater Magadha prepared and used drugs, often in ointments and plasters. What is more, the idea of restoring the balance of bodily fluids, central to classical Ayurveda, also appears to derive from the culture of Greater Magadha. As in the case of other cultural features (think of rebirth and karmic retribution), the medical tradition of Greater Magadha found its way into Brahmanical medicine and lived on as part of Ayurveda, whose very name (note the part -*veda*) bears testimony to the unjustified Brahmanical claim that this tradition was originally theirs.

The influence of Greater Magadha on the subsequent cultural and religious history of South Asia is hard to overestimate and may include many more features than the ones here enumerated. Unfortunately this culture left us virtually no textual sources apart from the Buddhist and Jaina canons so that it is extremely hard to find out more about it. Its major historical position was overshadowed in later centuries by the unprecedentedly successful spread of Brahmanism, to be discussed below. Here as elsewhere, Brahmanism reinterpreted past events, and even spread the idea that the creation of the Maurya empire (which had been a disaster for Brahmanism) was due to a Brahmanical advisor to its first emperor.

Jainism

One of the religious currents to appear in Greater Magadha in the middle of the first millennium B.C.E. was Jainism, and it is the one most apt to enlighten us on the problem of rebirth and karmic retribution. The reason is that it offered a solution that fits the problem like a glove. By studying its solution, we find out how exactly the problem was thought of.

The solution offered in the earliest Jaina texts (and confirmed in other early sources) is asceticism. Not just any kind of asceticism. Liberation was thought to be the end result of a long period of ascetic exertions, which culminated in the total immobilization of the ascetic. This immobilization concerned the body but also the mind. This immobilization went as far as it could possibly go, eventually including the suppression of activities such as breathing, and inevitably resulted in physical death. Indeed, liberation was thought to occur at the moment of death, provided that all other conditions had been fulfilled.

We will return to those other conditions in a minute but will first consider what link there could possibly be between immobility asceticism and the belief in rebirth and karmic retribution. This link can easily be discerned. Karmic retribution means that *my* future is determined by what *I* do. Deeds are central to this belief, and the Sanskrit word *karma* does indeed primarily mean *deed, activity.* If deeds lead to rebirth, and I don't want to be reborn, the obvious remedy is to abstain from all activity. This is what the early Jainas did.

Probably the earliest surviving detailed description of the road leading to liberation in the Jaina texts occurs in the so-called *Acaranga Sutra.* I will not present it here, for it is long and difficult. The main points are, however, clear. The ascetic who decides that he is ready for it takes up a position—lying, sitting, or standing—abstains from all food, and faces death with complete indifference. He starves to death in a state of total restraint with regard to all activity and movement. It is the culmination of a life of training and preparation.

Jainism and Its Canon

The founder of Jainism as we know it, Mahavira, was a contemporary of the Buddha and must have lived, like the latter, in the fifth century B.C.E. Buddhist sources indicate that he died before the Buddha. It appears that the two teachers were aware of each other's existence but never met.

Jaina tradition is no doubt correct in its claim that Jainism split up at an early date. The consequences of this split are visible today: Jainism survives in two divisions that disagree with each other on a number of points of theory and practice. One of these differences concerns the dress requirements of monks. This difference has given the two divisions their names: The monks of the Shvetambaras (dressed in white) wear white clothes; those of the Digambaras (dressed in space) wear no clothes whatsoever.

A further difference concerns the survival of the earliest texts, believed to include (among other things) Mahavira's words. According to the Digambaras, these earliest texts have not survived; according to the Shvetambaras, they have, though incompletely. But even the Shvetambaras admit that these early texts, or what remained of them, were not committed to writing until the fifth century C.E. Until that time they had presumably been preserved orally.

Theoretically the Shvetambara canon consists of three

parts: (1) The Purvas (old texts), (2) The Angas (limbs), and (3) The Angabahya (subsidiary canon). The Shvetambaras them-selves consider part 1 to be entirely lost and that the same is true of portions of part 2. Linguistic and other criteria justify the belief that some of the surviving texts in the canon (among them the *Acaranga* and the *Uttaradhyayana*) are considerably older than others.

For the modern scholar it is clear that many of the texts in-cluded in the Shvetambara canon belong to a period not far re-moved from the date at which these texts were written down. Only some of these texts (such as the *Acaranga* and the *Ut-taradhyayana*) may go back to a period closer to the time of Mahavira. Other texts, most notably the *Thananga* and the *Samavayanga,* present topics in numerical sequence; they are based on, and give expression to, lists of topics that were con-sidered important and that had been arranged in accordance with the number of items they contained. This is an interest-ing feature of the Jaina canon, for the Buddhist canon contains similar texts, which came to exert a profound influence on the development of Buddhist thought (see "The Buddhist Canon" below).

The unreliability of a large part of the Jaina canon (at least as far as information about the earliest period is concerned) is no doubt due to the lack of a strictly organized mnemonic tra-dition. In this respect Jainism differed a lot from Brahman-ism, where the mnemonic tradition was strong and implied intensive training from a young age onward. Buddhism, too, with the institution of a well-regulated monastic tradition, suc-ceeded much better in preserving its ancient texts.

The emphasis on restraint of activity and movement is not sur-prising. We read repeatedly in the *Acaranga* that suffering is the re-sult of activity: "He knows that all this suffering is born from ac-tivity"; "No action is found in him who has abandoned activity, the condition for rebirth originates on account of activity."

The most obvious remedy against such a situation is abstention from activity: "Free from activity he knows and sees, he does not long for anything because of his insight"; "He is wise and awakened who has ceased from activity.... Looking at those among the mortals in this world who are free from activity, having seen the result connected with activity, he who really knows turns away from activity"; and so forth.

All this gives us a clear and intelligible picture of the way to liberation in early Jainism. Activity being the source of all unhappiness, the monk tries to stop it in a most radical manner. The monk abstains from food and prepares for death in a position that is as motionless as possible.

The picture presented so far contains a serious flaw, and the early Jainas were aware of it. Given their beliefs, it cannot be denied that the abstention from all activity does not produce karmic consequences. However, before abstaining from all deeds, even the most committed Jaina ascetic has been active in the world, in his present life and even more so in the innumerable lives that he has lived before. All those earlier deeds will be clamoring for retribution, and the short time that our ascetic spends motionlessly will not change this. As a result, even the most extreme form of asceticism cannot lead to the desired end. The crucial question the Jaina practitioners were confronted with is how to disencumber themselves from the traces of their earlier deeds.

They had an answer. Immobility asceticism is not agreeable. Remaining in a standing position for days on end, preferably in the heat of the sun, abstaining from food and drink, not protecting one's body from stinging insects and other vermin that will prey upon the ascetic—all this creates great suffering. The Jainas looked upon this suffering not as an inevitable byproduct of the chosen method, but as an essential part of it. This suffering, they claimed, destroys the traces of earlier deeds.

Already the *Uttaradhyayana,* another early Jaina text, gives expression to this double role of asceticism. We read here, for example: "What does the soul produce by renouncing activity? By renouncing activity it produces a state without activity. By being without activity the soul does not bind new karma and destroys the karma that was bound before."

Note that this passage, along with many others, explicitly attributes a double function to immobility asceticism. On the one hand, the ascetic, for the very reason that he (or, more exceptionally, she) does not do anything, does nothing that could bring about karmic retribution. On the other, he burns the traces of earlier deeds. Asceticism, if judiciously practiced, may in this way culminate in a moment (the moment of bodily death of the ascetic) in which no karmic traces are left that might be the occasion for a new life. The ascetic, in this case, will not be reborn.

Interestingly, the early Buddhist texts, where they criticize the Jainas, attribute to them this same conviction of the double function of asceticism. The following passage, which presents the Buddha as being in conversation with a person named Mahanama, is of particular interest:

> At one time, Mahanama, I resided...on the mountain Gijjhakuta. At that time there were many Jainas on the black rock on the slope of the mountain Isigili, standing erect, refusing to sit down, and they experienced painful, sharp, severe sensations that were due to self-inflicted torture. Then, Mahanama, having arisen in the evening from my retirement, I went to...where those Jainas were; having gone there I said to those Jainas: "Why, dear Jainas, are you standing erect, refusing to sit down, and do you experience painful, sharp, severe sensations that are due to self-inflicted torture?" When this was said, Mahanama, those Jainas said to me: "Friend, the Jaina Nathaputta, who knows all and sees all, claims complete knowledge and insight saying: 'Always and continuously knowledge and insight are present to me, whether I walk, stand still, sleep or be awake.' He [i.e., Nathaputta] says: 'Formerly, Jainas, you performed sinful activities; you must exhaust that sinful activity by means of this severe and difficult practice. Being here and now restrained in body, speech, and mind amounts to not performing sinful activity in the future. Thus, as a result of the annihilation of former actions by asceticism and of the nonperforming of new actions, there is no further effect in the future; as a result of no further effect in the future there is destruction of actions; as a result of the destruction of actions there is destruction of suffer-

ing; as a result of the destruction of suffering there is destruction of sensation; as a result of the destruction of sensation all suffering will be exhausted.' And this word of Nathaputta pleases us and is approved of by us, and therefore we are delighted.... Happiness, dear Gotama, should not be reached through happiness; happiness should be reached through hardship."

The person called Nathaputta in this passage is the same as Mahavira, held to be the last omniscient saint of the Jainas. The Jainas, we learn from this passage, were "standing erect, refusing to sit down," and we are given to understand that they did so for the purpose of "the nonperforming of new actions" and "the annihilation of former actions by asceticism."

It will now be clear that serious Jaina ascetics should take care not to die too soon. If they died before they had experienced the required amount of suffering, traces of earlier deeds would remain, and they would be reborn. This explains why all conditions must be fulfilled before Jaina ascetics can decide that they are now ready for liberation, by means of a self-inflicted death induced by lack of food and exhaustion.

This, then, is the method proposed in the early Jaina sources. What does it teach us about the notion of rebirth and karmic retribution?

The answer is straightforward: The Jaina method is based upon the assumption that all activity—including involuntary activity, such as breathing—has karmic consequences and binds a person to the cycle of rebirths. All activity, it may be recalled, includes good deeds. Good deeds may secure a good rebirth. They get us no closer to the highest aim: liberation from rebirth. Morality has no role to play on the highest steps of the ladder to liberation in early Jainism.

The activity from which committed Jaina ascetics try to free themselves was not only bodily activity. Breathing, a bodily activity that is particularly difficult to stop, is part of it. But mental activity, too, should be stopped. The accomplished Jaina ascetic does not only physically resemble some kind of statue in the landscape. The mind, too, has come to a complete standstill. It has to be like this, for also thoughts and feelings have karmic consequences.

Ajivikism

Ajivikism is a vanished Indian religion, in the sense that it has no followers any longer. It arose roughly at the time of Jainism and Buddhism, in the same region, and survived for some two thousand years before it disappeared without leaving any literature of its own. There are reasons to think that it was quite popular in its early days (the great emperor Ashoka gave the Ajivikas a cave with an inscription to that effect in the third century B.C.E.). A close inspection of the sources of information about this religion that have survived confirm that it was indeed close to Jainism. Its ideas about rebirth and karmic retribution, in particular, differ only in one important respect from those of the early Jainas.

Remember that advanced Jaina practitioners pursued a double goal: (1) abstaining from all bodily and mental activity by means of immobilization asceticism; (2) destroying the traces of deeds performed in the past by means of the suffering brought about by that same immobility asceticism. Asceticism played in this manner a double role.

The Ajivikas agreed with the Jainas on all essential points but one. They, too, were of the opinion that all deeds, whether physical or mental, had consequences, usually in a future life. They also drew the conclusion that the only means not to create now the seeds for future lives was the abstention from all activity. They did not, however, accept that the suffering that necessarily accompanies such a radical immobilization destroys the traces of deeds performed in the past.

Their dilemma is manifest. How could they liberate themselves from the cycle of rebirths and karmic retribution if there was no way to destroy the traces of earlier deeds? The answer is simple: they could not. Liberation could not be forced. Traces of earlier deeds could not be suppressed. They would only go away once they had brought about their natural, karmic, consequences. But by the time they had done so, new acts would have been committed, which would leave traces of their own that would not go away until they too had brought about their karmic consequences. And so it would go on, birth after birth over endless periods of time.

The one, and relatively small, theoretical difference between Jainism and Ajivikism resulted thus in a major difference in practice. Jainism taught that there was a way to put an end to the cycle of rebirths, Ajivikism had to concede that there was not. For Ajivikism every individual would go on being born and reborn according to a fixed pattern from which there was no escape. The belief of the ordinary Ajivikas therefore amounted to a strict determinism or even fatalism, which left them no way to reach the highest goal: freedom from rebirth.

Our information about the Ajivikas is admittedly lacunary, primarily because no Ajivika texts have been preserved. There is, however, an enigmatic passage about Ajivika doctrine preserved in the Buddhist canon and confirmed in its essentials by information contained in the Jaina canon. This passage reads as follows in the paraphrase of A. L. Basham:

> There is neither cause nor basis for the sins of living beings; they become sinful without cause or basis. Neither is there cause or basis for the purity of living beings; they become pure without cause or basis. There is no deed performed either by oneself or by others, no human action, no strength, no courage, no human endurance or human prowess. All beings, all that have breath, all that are born, all that have life, are without power, strength, or virtue, but are developed by destiny, chance, and nature, and experience joy and sorrow in the six classes of existence. There are 1,400,000 chief uterine births...and 8,400,000 great world periods [kalpa] through which fool and wise alike will take their course, and make an end of sorrow. There is no question of bringing unripe karma to fruition, nor of exhausting karma already ripened, by virtuous conduct, by vows, by penance, or by chastity. That cannot be done. The cycle of rebirths [samsara] is measured as with a bushel, with its joy and sorrow and its appointed end. It can neither be lessened nor increased, nor is there any excess or deficiency of it. Just as a ball of thread will, when thrown, unwind to its full length, so fool and wise alike will take their course, and make an end of sorrow.

The passage contains parts that are difficult to understand, some of which have been omitted here. However, the central point of Ajivikism is clearly expressed: there is no such thing as discarding past karma by any other means than experiencing its consequences.

However, even the dark clouds of Ajivikism had a silver lining. The cycle of rebirths, the Ajivikas believed, was not endless. It covered a long time, to be sure; 8,400,000 kalpas is a long time indeed. Given that each kalpa covers many millions of years, it is easy to see that the full number of years in a complete "life cycle" is astronomical. (A duration of 4,320 million years is sometimes advanced for a kalpa; 8,400,000 kalpas will in that case correspond to more than thirty five quadrillion [35×10^{15}] years, far longer than the modern astronomical estimate of the age of the universe with its "mere" 13.7 billion [13.7×10^{9}] years.) But yet, there is going to be an end. Those who have come to the end, how will they behave? The answer, which we have learned from Jainism, is clear. Such people will practice immobility asceticism. They do so, in this case, not in order to reach liberation, but *because* they are about to attain liberation. The distinction is subtle but not unknown in other religions: Calvinists claimed that they lived virtuous lives not in order to be saved, but because they had been predestined to be saved.

Ajivikism was preached by people who lived ascetic lives because they were sure that they had come to the end of their time. They succeeded in converting people to their views, but most of those converts, naturally, did not become ascetics themselves, but limited themselves to accepting a strictly deterministic world view. It is possible that such a world view suited them well in a world that increasingly emphasized the fixed position that each individual occupied, and had to occupy, in society, as we will see below. We do not know for sure, and we never will, as no texts belonging to this religion have survived. We will see, however, that other sources (including the *Mahabharata*, a famous Sanskrit epic dating from the last centuries preceding the Common Era) are acquainted with forms of fatalism, which they do not, however, associate with the name Ajivikism.

Before we leave Ajivikism, it will be useful to have a closer look at the fatalism it preaches. For the doctrine to make sense, it must be assumed that previous deeds determine the present completely or almost completely. Most in particular, previous deeds determine our present deeds, which in their turn determine our fate in a next life.

There is no possibility of escape because we are in no position to resist our karmic pressure from the past. Only in this way can it be maintained that the full series of births and rebirths is determined from the beginning and that the number and nature of life forms everyone has to pass through is fixed.

There is no logical necessity to the belief that earlier deeds determine every last detail of subsequent lives even if we accept that they do play a major role in this process. It is easy to imagine a situation in which a person, though under great karmic pressure, decides to resist this pressure and act in accordance with his or her own judgment. Many religious thinkers of India did indeed take this position, leaving to individuals at least some freedom to act in ways that were not completely predetermined by their earlier deeds. However, the deterministic current remained strong, too, and finds expression variously in the early texts. We will come across an example in our discussion of the *Bhagavadgita* below.

Knowledge of the Self

The clear and straightforward understanding of the nature of karma that we find in early Jainism was not confined to that religion. Exactly the same notion, and therefore the same problem, was associated with a different solution. To understand this other solution, we have to think, here too, of karmic retribution as concerning all forms of activity, bodily as well as mental. And in the case of this other solution, too, moral considerations play no central role.

Consider the following disagreement someone might have with the early Jainas: You, Jainas, have correctly understood that your deeds—all deeds, whatever their nature—are responsible for your future lives. To avoid rebirth, you have decided to desist from all forms of activity. But what you do is forcing your body and your mind to stop acting. In so doing, you identify with your body and your mind. You appear to think that what your body and your mind do is what *you* do. But how can you be so sure that you are your body and your mind?

The critic who formulated these questions did, as a matter of fact, have ideas of his own as to his real nature. Far from looking upon himself as being identical with his body and his mind, he was convinced that his real self was different from both. This real self, aside from being different from body and mind, never acts. And being inactive by its very nature, it is not affected by the deeds carried out by body and mind. These deeds of body and mind continue the cycle of rebirth and karmic retribution, to be sure. But that is because the person concerned is ignorant about his true nature. Knowledge of the inherently inactive nature of the real self, once acquired, changes the situation. Once fully realized, it frees the person from the consequences of deeds that he has in reality never carried out.

It should be noted that the entity here referred to as "self" is altogether different from what this word may refer to in different cultures. Indeed, one of the Indian terms used to designate it (though not the only one) is *atman*. Like *self* in English, *atman* is (or can be used as) a reflexive pronoun, as in "He gave himself a holiday." This is the reason for the choice of "self" in this context, even though the English "self" is probably never thought of as an inactive entity. Some translators prefer other words, such as "soul," but this seems to me even more prone to misunderstandings. Whatever the translation chosen, it is vital to remember that it refers to a notion altogether different from any notion current in the modern Western world. (Something remotely similar was found in Christian Gnosticism; see Concluding Comments at the end of this book.)

Knowledge of the true nature of the self becomes an oft-recurring theme in Indian religious thought. This self was thought of in various ways: some thought it was pure consciousness, others added bliss, others again took both away and stated that the true self was as unconscious as a stone. But all agreed on one thing: the true self never acts. And this was crucial because this feature of the self turned knowledge of the self into a prerequisite for liberation from the cycle of rebirth and karmic retribution.

Are we entitled to suspect that this particular concept of the self was invented to suit the purposes of those who wished to escape from the effects of karma but were not ready to engage in the extreme forms of asceticism practiced by the Jainas? It is true that we find this concept of the self in India almost exclusively in connection with the belief in rebirth and karmic retribution. However, very similar concepts of the self occur in religions elsewhere in the world, in contexts where the belief in rebirth and karmic retribution is not found. This is not the place for a survey of those comparable concepts in other religions. Their very existence should warn us against drawing too rapid, and too glib, conclusions. It seems highly unlikely that the notion of an inactive self was invented by spiritual seekers who wanted to avoid the hardships of immobility asceticism. The opposite view— that the belief in rebirth and karmic retribution was invented by people who thought that their real self was inactive by nature—is not justified either. Beliefs like these are not "invented" by clever schemers who calculate their advantage. In spite of this, a case could be made that the different notions involved—karmic retribution, an inactive self, immobilization as spiritual practice—belong together and have always belonged together. This does not help us much in finding out how the notion of karma with all that implies came about in India, but it does arm us against simplistic theories that treat beliefs like this as isolated elements that could be transferred from one culture to another the way commercial objects can be traded. (Further reflections about the coexistence of these notions will be found at the very end of this book.)

The notion of an inactive self became extremely popular in India. Most of the Brahmanical philosophies adopted it, and their ontologies may be looked upon as theoretical constructs built around this notion. More will be said about this in a later chapter. Here we must first turn to another religious current that originated in the region in which Jainism arose and see how it came to terms with the belief in rebirth and karmic retribution.

Buddhism

Ajivikism could only be understood against the background of Jainism. In order to understand Buddhism, we need to know about both Jainism and the currents that emphasized the role of knowledge of the self for gaining liberation.

Early Buddhism rejected both. It rejected immobility asceticism as a method to attain liberation, and it rejected knowledge of the true nature of the self as such a means. It could reject both because it accepted a different notion of karma, that is, of karmic retribution.

In early Buddhism, the cause of rebirth is not deeds, but desire;

indeed, the word *karma* and its cognates are not prominently used in its texts in this particular sense. Buddhist teaching is often presented in a nutshell in the form of the Four Noble Truths: the noble truth of suffering, the noble truth of the origin of suffering, the noble truth of the cessation of suffering, and the noble truth of the path that leads to the cessation of suffering. These Four Noble Truths are explained as follows:

This is the noble truth of *suffering:* Birth is suffering, old age is suffering, sickness is suffering, death is suffering, to be united with the unloved is suffering, to be separated from the loved is suffering, not to obtain what one desires is suffering; in short the fivefold clinging to the earthly is suffering.

This is the noble truth of the *origin of suffering:* it is the thirst for being that leads from birth to birth, together with lust and de-sire, which finds gratification here and there: the thirst for plea-sures, the thirst for being, the thirst for nonexistence.

This is the noble truth of the *cessation of suffering:* the cessa-tion of this thirst by the complete annihilation of desire, letting it go, expelling it, separating oneself from it, giving it no room.

This is the noble truth of the *path that leads to the cessation of suffering:* it is this Noble Eightfold Path: to wit, Right Faith, Right Resolve, Right Speech, Right Action, Right Living, Right Effort, Right Thought, Right Concentration.

It is clear from this passage that Buddhism psychologized the no-tion of karmic retribution. Indeed, the *Dhammapada* (1.1–2), an early Buddhist text, puts it like this:

All things are led by thought, are controlled by thought, are made up by thought. If one speaks or acts with malevolent thought, then suffering follows one, just as the wheel follows the foot of an ox.

All things are led by thought, are controlled by thought, are made up by thought. If one speaks or acts with benevolent thought, then happiness follows one, just as a shadow does not leave.

Occasionally karma is also identified with intention.

The Buddhist Canon

Apart from Vedic literature, the Buddhist canon has preserved some of the earliest texts of South Asia. The Buddhist tradition ascribes many of these texts, though not all of them, to the Buddha himself, but this claim has to be treated with caution, for it is clear that the Buddhist canon had grown for a long time before it reached the more or less fixed character in which we now know it.

The Buddhist canon is known by the name Tripitaka because it consists of three *(tri)* baskets *(pitaka)*. One of these three baskets, the *Vinaya-pitaka*, deals with monastic discipline *(vinaya)* and is supposed to contain the rules pronounced by the Buddha. The second basket, the *Sutra-pitaka*, contains the discourses *(sutra)* believed to have been uttered by the Buddha or occasionally one of his disciples. The third basket, finally, is called *Abhidharma-pitaka* because it deals with Abhidharma, a form of Buddhist scholasticism that belongs to a more recent period. Only the second basket, the *Sutra-pitaka*, provides us with material regarding the teachings of early Buddhism.

Already the *Sutra-pitaka* manifests—in its internal arrangement and in the contents of certain sutras—the tendency to create lists of items that were considered important in Buddhist teaching. These lists subsequently became the basis for the scholastic developments that find expression in the *Abhidharma-pitaka*, and for the creation of Buddhist systematic philosophy (see the boxed text titled "Buddhist Scholasticism and the Beginning of Indian Philosophy" below).

The dates when the Buddha lived are not precisely known, but much recent research justifies the conclusion that he may have died around 400 B.C.E., give or take a few decades. The Buddhist canon, in contrast, did not reach its final form until many centuries later, and additions and modification may still have been made during the early centuries C.E. A first written version was produced in Sri Lanka during the first century B.C.E.

The early Buddhists preserved their texts, orally, in the languages of the regions in which they lived. Buddhists in different parts of the subcontinents therefore preserved their texts in different languages. The Buddhists of Sri Lanka, for example, preserved their texts in a language that in recent centuries came to be known as Pali, but which they thought was Magadhi, the language of Magadha, the region where the Buddha had preached. Scholars have been able to show that Pali was really a language of western India (and therefore not from Magadha, which lies in the east), no doubt because Sri Lanka received Buddhism from western India. The Tripitaka in Pali has been preserved in its entirety.

The Buddhists of the subcontinent adopted, from the first or second century C.E. onward, the Sanskrit language and translated their sacred texts into this language. This explains that bits and pieces of the early Buddhist texts have also survived in Sanskrit. Since Buddhism disappeared from the Indian subcontinent soon after the year 1000 C.E., very few of its scriptures have survived there. However, the spread of Buddhism into China from the early centuries C.E. on had the consequence that numerous early Buddhist texts were translated into Chinese. Texts belonging to the properly Indian schools of Buddhism have therefore survived in that language.

The Buddhists, then, believed that rebirth could be prevented not by the destruction of all deeds, but by the destruction of the roots of all desire. Destroying the roots of desire is different from stopping activity. The Buddhist method was therefore altogether different from the Jaina one. Rather than practicing immobility asceticism, Buddhists in search of liberation would try to bring about psychological changes in themselves by means of exercises designed to help them in this endeavor.

Given this different notion of karmic retribution, knowledge of the true nature of the self as inactive does not help much either. Passages in the ancient discourses express themselves to that extent.

Their formulation is unfortunately such that many later Buddhists, as well as a number of modern scholars, have misunderstood them, thinking that these passages deny the existence of the self rather than its role in gaining liberation.

In an important and frequently recurring passage, the Buddha is presented as contrasting the constituent part of a human person as conceived of by him with the notion of a self. These constituent parts are the five aggregates: (1) the body *(rupa)*, (2) the sensations *(vedana)*, (3) the ideations *(sanjna)*, (4) the conditioned factors *(samskara)*, and (5) consciousness *(vijnana)*. The Buddha said the following about them:

> "The body [*rupa*] is not the self. For if the body were the self, the body would not give rise to affliction, and one should be able to say: 'Let my body be thus and so; let my body not be thus and so.' But because the body is not the self, the body gives rise to affliction, and one cannot say: 'Let my body be thus and so; let my body not be thus and so.'
>
> The sensations [*vedana*] are not the self. . . . Ideations [*sanjna*] are not the self. . . . The conditioned factors [*samskara*] are not the self. . . . Consciousness [*vijnana*] is not the self. For if consciousness were the self, consciousness would not give rise to affliction, and one should be able to say: 'Let consciousness be thus and so, let consciousness not be thus and so.' But because consciousness is not the self, consciousness gives rise to affliction, and one cannot say: 'Let consciousness be thus and so, let consciousness not be thus and so.'"
>
> "What do you think, monks, is the body permanent or impermanent?"
>
> "Impermanent, sir."
>
> "Is that which is impermanent suffering or happiness?"
>
> "Suffering, sir."
>
> "Is that which is impermanent, suffering, and subject to change fit to be regarded thus: 'This is mine, this is I, this is my self?'"
>
> "No, sir."
>
> "Are sensations permanent or impermanent? . . . Are ideations permanent or impermanent? . . . Are the conditioned factors per-

manent or impermanent?...Is consciousness permanent or impermanent?"

"Impermanent, sir."

"Is that which is impermanent suffering or happiness?"

"Suffering, sir."

"Is that which is impermanent, suffering, and subject to change fit to be regarded thus: 'This is mine, this is I, this is my self?'"

"No, sir."

"Therefore, monks, the body, the sensations, the ideations, the conditioned factors, consciousness should be seen for what they really are: 'This is not mine, this is not I, this is not my self.'"

This passage reveals a clear notion of the self: it is permanent, bliss, not subject to change. This notion shares the features of permanence and unchangeability with the self conceived of by those who think that knowledge of that self is crucial for attaining liberation. (Indeed, some add bliss to this list of characteristics of the self.) The Buddhist texts know the notion but do not consider knowledge of such a self important. The above passage does not state that a self of that nature does or does not exist, and the same is true of other canonical passages. The existence of such a self is passed over in silence, but the soteriological significance of knowing such a self is rejected.

If, then, Buddhism rejected both immobility asceticism and knowledge of the true (immobile) nature of the self as means to gain freedom from rebirth and karmic retribution, did it think that liberation was possible at all? Ajivikism had no method and had no better advice for its spiritual seekers than that they had to wait, perhaps for an inconceivably long period of time. Like Ajivikism, Buddhism rejected the two methods that we have considered so far. Did it have a method of its own, or did it tell its followers to give up all hope?

Buddhism did have a method of its own. Given the way it conceived of karmic retribution, it is even possible to predict what kind of method this was. Since desire is the cause of rebirth, liberation of rebirth can be attained through the destruction of desire. Desire, however, is a psychological phenomenon. The destruction of desire is not to be identified with the restraint of desire. Restraint characterized the asceticism of the Jainas. Buddhism proposed to dig deeper, at least where desire is concerned. It taught a path leading to the annihilation of desire, or at any rate it claimed to do so.

How does one destroy one's desires? The question is a lot more difficult to answer (at least theoretically) than the question how one stops activity. Stopping activity is straightforward, even if infinitely difficult in practice. But even in mere theory it is not obvious how one could destroy one's desires. Destroying desire is yet a centerpiece of Buddhist teaching. It is hardly surprising that an important part of the ancient Buddhist canon consists of descriptions of various psychological practices that ultimately are supposed to lead to that end.

Clearly the path taught by the Buddha is a psychological path. Those who follow the path engage in a number of psychological practices of different kinds. Some parts of the ancient canon concentrate on some chosen practices, more or less in isolation from the other ones, which makes it at first sight difficult to get an overview of the path in its entirety. Fortunately there is one relatively long passage that occurs numerous times in the ancient texts and that presents a complete sketch—from beginning to end, so to say—of the path. It describes the steps taken by someone who hears the teachings of the Buddha, is convinced by them, and decides to follow them to the letter. He leaves society and avoids all forms of interaction with others that might divert his attention, cultivating peace and contentment. This is, however, only the beginning of what follows. Once this man (note that the passage concerned only speaks of men and that it is indeed uncertain whether the Buddha accepted nuns during his lifetime) has developed peace and contentment and discarded causes of friction, he turns to practicing awareness of all he does. This practice, known as *smriti* in Sanskrit, *sati* in Pali, henceforth accompanies all (that means every single thing) our adept does. It is, as a matter of fact, the background and condition for what follows. What follows is what is called meditation (*dhyana* in Sanskrit, *jhana* in Pali). This meditation is presented as consisting of four stages, beginning with a complete disengagement from the world and characterized by complete equanimity and an ever deeper state of absorption. Meditation itself does not by itself lead to the goal. The destruction of desire, or rather of the "taints" that are the roots of desire, takes place in the deepest state of absorption. It is hard to extract from the texts what exactly the meditator does in this deepest stage of absorption, but it is clear that he directs his concentrated mind in a way that results in the removal of those "taints." Once this is done, the meditator knows that he has succeeded, that he is liberated, that he has arrived at the end of suffering.

One might reasonably ask how and why the practice of meditation should lead to the end of rebirth and karmic retribution. Unlike the link between, say, immobility asceticism and liberation from rebirth, the link between meditative practices and liberation is far from self-evident. The connecting factor is desire. A link between meditative practices and the destruction of desire, whether real or imagined, makes sense: if one wishes to change one's psychological constitution, a psychological method seems appropriate. Liberation from rebirth follows from the destruction of desire because desire is the force that brings about karmic retribution.

In spite of these considerations, the belief that desire rather than activity is responsible for karmic retribution is not evident. Its remedy in the form of a psychological operation, too, does not share the simplicity and straightforwardness of its competitor, stopping all activity. Buddhism therefore had some explaining to do to make clear why desire should lead to karmic retribution. What is more, it seems likely that among the early converts there were many who, though willing to accept the preeminence of the Buddha, were loath to abandon their conviction that activity, and the control of activity, were key players in the process that leads to karmic retribution and to its cessation respectively.

These two factors were responsible for certain important developments. One of these is the following. Buddhism reveals itself from an early date onward highly susceptible to influences from outside, primarily from the milieu to which Jainism belonged. This leads to the peculiar situation that the same ascetic practices are sometimes criticized and sometimes prescribed in the early Buddhist texts. Also the cultivation of mental states whose main purpose is the cessation of all mental activity is sometimes rejected, sometimes recommended. Buddhism, in brief, comes to unite elements that originally belonged to altogether different currents of thought. Let us look at this more closely.

We know that early Buddhism distinguished itself from the other religious movement of Greater Magadha in various respects, most notably in its different conception of karma, and as a result in the different path it taught to attain liberation. The Buddhist path was, if not harder to practice, more difficult to understand. Indeed, why should complicated mental practices be all that is required to put an end to rebirth? If rebirth results from karma, one would expect that the end of rebirth will result from the suppression of karma, of deeds, whether literally through the suppression of all bodily and mental activity, or through the realization that the core of one's being, one's self, never acts and is incapable of acting. Early Buddhism taught neither of these two, and we can be sure that more than one early listener to the Buddhist message felt confused and failed to understand the connection between the problem and its presumed remedy.

The Buddhist canon has left ample traces of this confusion. It contains as a matter of fact a disturbing number of different precepts that are all attributed to the Buddha. These precepts are regularly in conflict with each other, so much so that it is necessary in a number of cases to conclude that teachings altogether different from those of the Buddha somehow found their way into the ancient canon. And more than once it is possible to identify those nonauthentic precepts as belonging to those religious currents of Greater Magadha in which suppression of all activity or identification of the core of one's being as inactive played a central role.

Consider the non-Buddhist notion that knowledge of the inactive nature of one's true self is an essential (perhaps even sufficient) condition for liberation from the effects of one's deeds. Buddhism rejects this notion in the famous passage studied above, which shows that none of the five main constituents of the person are such a self. However, another passage turns all this on its head by emphasizing that knowledge of the fact that all constituents of the (active) person are not the self is a condition for liberation. The liberating knowledge of the self of the non-Buddhists has in this way become a liberating knowledge of the not-self for the same reason: one disidentifies with the active parts of the person. Here we find a rejected non-Buddhist doctrine that has found its way, in a slightly modified form, into the Buddhist tradition.

Also the non-Buddhist notion that cessation of activity was a prerequisite for liberation exerted a strong attraction on certain Buddhists. This is clear from the fact that practices of that nature have found their way into the Buddhist canon. Most of these practices concern the immobilization of the mind and of the senses. Beside passages in which the Buddha ridicules the immobilization of the senses by stating that if that is the aim, the blind and deaf will be performing these practices, there are others in which he boasts not to have noticed a thing even though he found himself in the middle of a thunderstorm that killed, through lightning, several people and animals close to him.

Examples of such contradictions can easily be multiplied. They help us to identify nonauthentic elements in the Buddhist canon. Recall, for example, that the Jaina method of asceticism could be characterized as "the nonperforming of new actions" and "the annihilation of former actions by asceticism." The Buddha is regularly depicted as criticizing this path, and on one occasion he even makes fun of it, saying: "If the pleasure and pain that beings feel are caused by what was done in the past, then the Jainas surely must have done bad deeds in the past, since they now feel such painful, racking, piercing feelings." Elsewhere in the canon, however, he is presented as saying the opposite, recommending his listeners to carry out no fresh action and to wear out their former actions. Here the Jaina method is described not in order to criticize it, but as the method taught by the Buddha. Clearly this nonauthentic practice was introduced into the Buddhist canon, perhaps by followers who had never fully grasped the difference between the Buddhist and the Jaina methods.

Probably the most important among these nonauthentic elements are certain meditational states that are sometimes rejected but elsewhere presented as essential elements on the path to enlightenment. Most of the canonical passages (presumably the authentic ones) mention four meditational states, called *dhyana* in Sanskrit, *jhana* in Pali. Other texts add a number of further states that are never called *dhyana/jhana* but carry altogether different names. Among these additional states, often five in number, we find the "realm of nothingness" and the "realm of neither ideation nor nonideation." The series culminates in the "cessation of ideation and feeling." These names reveal that the emphasis in these additional states, unlike the states called *dhyana/jhana,* is on the suppression of thoughts and other mental activities. This aim—the suppression of all mental activities— has its place in the more general aim to suppress all activities what- soever, an aim that we have come to associate with the Jainas and perhaps other non-Buddhist ascetic movement of Greater Magadha. Unlike the *dhyanas/jhanas,* they do not lead to a higher goal (such as the destruction of the taints), and we may be sure that these medita- tional states, too, found their way into the Buddhist canon from out- side and cannot be looked upon as authentic teachings of the Bud- dha. With only one exception known to me, they are indeed never mentioned in accounts of the Buddha's enlightenment. Yet they have found a place in the story of the Buddha's death: the Buddha is sup- posed to have passed through the four *dhyanas* and the five addi- tional states before he finally expired in the fourth *dhyana.*

Another question that Buddhism had to answer is the follow- ing. Buddhism had to provide a theoretical justification for why de- sire has karmic consequences. A list of twelve elements illustrating "dependent origination" is usually assumed to fulfill this task. The list is, however, obscure (already a canonical text states that it is ex- tremely difficult to understand). Later theoreticians are faced with the challenge to throw further light on it, which they do with a lim- ited amount of success. It is possible to speculate that the tendency to theorize that accompanies Buddhism in subsequent centuries owes at least some of its impetus to this challenge that lies at the basis of the Buddhist attempts at understanding karmic retribution.

If we now turn to the practical role the belief in rebirth and karmic retribution played in the life of ordinary Buddhists, we may assume that Buddhism followed Jainism and Ajivikism in holding karma re- sponsible for many of the differences that distinguish people from each other, including differences in social status. The following pas- sage from the *Majjhima Nikaya* (3, pp. 202–203) illustrates this:

> "Master Gotama, what is the cause and condition why human be- ings are seen to be inferior and superior? For people are seen to be short-lived and long-lived, sickly and healthy, ugly and beau- tiful, uninfluential and influential, poor and wealthy, low-born

and high-born, stupid and wise. What is the cause and condition, Master Gotama, why human beings are seen to be inferior and superior?"

"Student, beings are owners of their actions, heirs of their actions; they originate from their actions, are bound to their actions, have their actions as their refuge. It is action that distinguishes beings as inferior and superior."

Note that this passage does not mention the Brahmanical division of society into four classes: Brahmins, Kshatriyas (warriors), Vaishyas, and Shudras. As a matter of fact, the early Buddhist texts do not normally speak about this Brahmanical division of society because they feel critical toward it. However, occasionally they do mention it in connection with karmic retribution, as in the following passage from the *Samyutta Nikaya* (1, pp. 93–94):

There are these four kinds of persons found existing in the world. What four? The one heading from darkness to darkness, the one heading from darkness to light, the one heading from light to darkness, the one heading from light to light.

And how is a person one heading from darkness to darkness? Here some person has been reborn in a low family—a family of untouchables, bamboo workers, hunters, cartwrights, or flower scavengers—a poor family in which there is little food and drink and which subsists with difficulty, one where food and clothing are obtained with difficulty; and he is ugly, unsightly, deformed, chronically ill—purblind or cripple-handed or lame or paralyzed. He is not one who gains food, drink, clothing, and vehicles; garlands, scents, and unguents; bedding, housing, and lighting. He engages in misconduct of body, speech, and mind. Having done so, with the breakup of the body, after death, he is reborn in the plane of misery, in a bad destination, in the nether world, in hell....

And how is a person one heading from darkness to light? Here some person has been reborn in a low family...one where food and clothing are obtained with difficulty; and he is ugly...or paralyzed. He is not one who gains food...and lighting. He engages in good conduct of body, speech, and mind. Having done so, with

the breakup of the body, after death, he is reborn in a good destination, in a heavenly world....

And how is a person one heading from light to darkness? Here
some person has been reborn in a high family—an affluent warrior family, an affluent Brahmin family, or an affluent householder family—one that is rich, with great wealth and property,
with abundant gold and silver, abundant treasures and commodi-
ties, abundant wealth and grain; and he is handsome, attractive,
graceful, possessing supreme beauty of complexion. He is one who
gains food, drink, clothing, and vehicles; garlands, scents, and unguents; bedding, housing, and lighting. He engages in misconduct
of body, speech, and mind. Having done so, with the breakup of
the body, after death, he is reborn in the plane of misery, in a bad
destination, in the nether world, in hell....

And how is a person one heading from light to light? Here some
person has been reborn in a high family...with abundant wealth
and grain; and he is handsome, attractive, graceful, possessing
supreme beauty of complexion. He is one who gains food...and
lighting. He engages in good conduct of body, speech, and mind.
Having done so, with the breakup of the body, after death, he is
reborn in a good destination, in a heavenly world.

Brahmins and warriors *(kshatriya),* two of the four regular Brahmanical classes of society, are explicitly mentioned in this passage,
as are outcasts *(candala),* another Brahmanical designation. Interestingly, none of these are presented as the outcome of earlier deeds. It is
as if the author of this passage was loath to use the doctrine of karma
as a justification for a division of society about which the Buddhists
felt very critical.

CHAPTER 3

Karma in Brahmanism

During the period in which Jainism, Buddhism, and Ajivikism arose, Brahmanism belonged primarily to a geographically limited area, with its heartland in the middle and western parts of the Ganges plain. It was in this region that Brahmanism had been the culture of a largely hereditary class of priests, the Brahmins, who derived their livelihood and special position in society from their close association with the local rulers. These same Brahmins memorized and preserved the Veda, a large corpus of literature concerned primarily with their sacrificial activities (see the boxed text below).

This situation changed with the political unification of northern India, begun by the Nandas and continued by the Mauryas (fourth to second centuries B.C.E.). Both the Nandas and the Mauryas had their home base in Magadha (to the east of the Brahmanical heartland) and had no particular interest in Brahmins and their sacrificial tradition. As a result Brahmanism as an institution was under threat; it had to either face disappearance or reinvent itself. It did the latter. Brahmanism underwent a transformation that enabled it to survive and ultimately flourish in changed circumstances.

Brahmanism had been a priestly religion with heavy emphasis on elaborate sacrifices. The transformed Brahmanism that in due time succeeded in spreading all over the Indian subcontinent and into Southeast Asia was primarily (though not exclusively) a sociopolitical ideology. Brahmanism had clear ideas about the correct hierarchical order of society (with the Brahmins at the top) and the correct manner of running a state. Brahmanism had not abandoned its elaborate sacrificial heritage, to be sure, but now came to include less elaborate (and sometimes totally unconnected) forms of religious practice. In this way it could adjust to a variety of religious cults, with one nonnegotiable condition: Brahmins were the ones most suited to establish and maintain links with "higher" realms; they were the ones to advise rulers on social and political matters; and they were the ones to occupy the highest place in the social hierarchy.

The outcome of this Brahmanical transformation was quite extraordinary. A thousand years after the establishment of the Maurya empire (presumably a catastrophe for the Brahmins), Brahmanical sociopolitical ideology predominated in an immense geographical area, reaching from Vietnam and Indonesia at one end to western India at the other. This dominating presence found expression in various ways, including the use of Sanskrit, the sacred language of Brahmanism, in political inscriptions, in courtly literature, and even in an important part of the literature of Buddhism and Jainism. The American researcher Sheldon Pollock has coined the term "Sanskrit cosmopolis" to designate this phenomenon.

The long-term success of Brahmanism was at least in part due to the literary and conceptual tools its adherents had developed during the final centuries B.C.E. Among their most powerful conceptual tools we must count their vision of society: how it was and how it should be. Brahmanism proposed (and in the long run imposed) a division of society into four or more layers, each with its own tasks and obligations. It appears that other inhabitants of the subcontinent (with the notable exception of the Greeks at its northwestern margins) had not elaborated ideas of their own as to the structure and organization of society. Debates about such issues, with Buddhists or others, were therefore necessarily conducted in Brahmanical terms: the Brahmins "framed" the debate and naturally came out victoriously. Outsiders might have ideas of their own as to what constitutes a "true" Brahmin or claim that the hierarchical order of the two topmost layers (Brahmins and warriors) should be reversed; the very fact that they formulated their objections in Brahmanical terms secured the ultimate victory of the Brahmanical scheme of things.

Brahmanism also created a number of literary tools during the final centuries B.C.E. These texts address two different audiences:

other Brahmins and outsiders. The texts by Brahmins for Brahmins were mainly concerned with rules of behavior that would secure a separate identity for the Brahmins. These texts rarely deal with issues related to rebirth and karmic retribution. Other texts were also meant for a wider audience. Among these we must count the Sanskrit epics. These texts, the *Mahabharata* in particular, had to deal with issues that were alive in the non-Brahmanical populations that Brahmanism had to confront, among these rebirth and karmic retribution. The *Mahabharata* shows in a number of places how Brahmanism came to terms with those external beliefs by trying to incorporate them in a broader Brahmanical vision. It is therefore a source of information with regard to originally non-Brahmanical customs and beliefs but one that has to be read with great care, precisely because those non-Brahmanical customs and beliefs appear here in Brahmanized form.

Absence in Vedic Literature

Turning first to Vedic literature, it is clear that this literature was already old when Buddhism and the other currents we have considered came into existence. This literature contains no trace of the notion of rebirth and karmic retribution. The few hints at a belief in rebirth that some scholars have brought to light are not accompanied by a belief in karmic retribution. A belief in rebirth, unlike the belief in karmic retribution, is widespread in the world. The conclusion is justified that the antecedents of rebirth and karmic retribution (combined) are not to be sought in Vedic literature.

The Veda

The term *Veda* designates a large corpus of literature that contains texts composed over a period of many centuries: the oldest portions may have been composed well before the year 1000 B.C.E., while its most recent portions may be more than a millennium more recent. The Veda constitutes the sacred literary heritage of the Brahmins and is for the most part concerned with the sacrifices that could only be carried out with the assistance of Brahmin priests. A considerable part of the Vedic corpus consists of sacred formulas, called mantras in Sanskrit, that had to be recited at sacrifices and other solemn events. Most of the remainder contains a variety of myths, reflections, and speculations about those sacrifices. Sometimes, especially in those relatively recent portions known by the name Upanishads (presumably more recent than the founders of Jainism and Buddhism), speculation goes beyond the sacrifice and deals with more general "mystical" issues. The frequently made claim that the Upanishads give expression to mystical experiences remains for the time being unsubstantiated.

Beside the word *Veda* in the singular, it is also common to speak of four Vedas: the one Vedic corpus is then thought of as consisting of four Vedas, that is, the *Rigveda,* the *Samaveda,* the *Yajurveda,* and the *Atharvaveda.* These different Vedas are associated with different Brahmin priests, who play different parts in the performance of major sacrifices.

Most Vedic texts were composed orally by authors who were not acquainted with writing. They were subsequently preserved in the same way, orally. Certain parts of the Veda—most notably the collection of mantras of the *Rigveda,* with its 400,000 syllables considerably bigger than the New Testament—have been preserved orally to this day. Students took (and to some extent still take) a long time to memorize "their" Veda, traditionally twelve years for one Veda, forty-eight years for those ambitious enough to wish to learn them all by heart. The emphasis was (and still is) on the exact repetition of the form of the mantras, not on the understanding of their meaning. This is not surprising given that the efficacy of these sacred formulas depends on their correct pronunciation, not on the understanding of the reciter.

It is not clear when Vedic texts were written down for the first time. The Brahmanical tradition has always maintained that the "real" Veda is the recited Veda, not a written version of it. As recently as the year 1000 C.E., the Persian traveler Alberuni wrote: "The Brahmins recite the Veda without understanding its meaning, and in the same way they learn it by heart, the one receiving it from the other. Only a few of them learn its explanation, and still less is the number of those who master the contents of the Veda and their interpretation to such a degree as to be able to hold a theological disputation.... They do not allow the Veda to be committed to writing, because it is recited according to certain modulations, and they therefore avoid the use of the pen, since it is liable to cause some error and may occasion an addition or a defect in the written text. In consequence it has happened that they have several times forgotten the Veda and lost it." Alberuni then reports that, not long before his time, a Brahmin from Kashmir had committed the Veda to writing out of fear that it might be forgotten.

For modern scholarship, the Veda is a source of information about the period during which it was composed and most specifically about its religious ideas and practices. Unfortunately it is not clear when exactly the different parts of the Veda were composed. It has long been taken for granted (or rather argued on the basis of invalid arguments) that the whole Vedic corpus preceded the time of the Buddha (who appears to have died soon after 400 B.C.E.). This position may now have to be abandoned. It is becoming clear, for example, that a Middle Vedic text such as the *Aitareya Brahmana* is composed in a language that is closer to the language described by the grammarian Panini (350 B.C.E. or later) than any other text. The two major Upanishads—the *Brihadaranyaka* and the *Chandogya*—must be more recent, and this can indeed be supported with strong independent arguments for the former of these two, which may not have reached anything like its present form until after Patañjali, another grammarian, who lived in the middle of the second century B.C.E. Another Upanishad that used to be assigned to an unrealistically early date, the *Shvetashvatara Upanishad,* appears to be more recent than the *Bhagavadgita* and to belong to the early centuries C.E.

Vedic literature was the exclusive property of Brahmins. Inevitably Brahmins came in contact with the belief in rebirth and karmic retribution. In order to understand how they reacted, it is necessary to know more about their tradition.

One of the most central claims of Brahmanism is that there is a hierarchical order of human beings. There is a fundamental division into four classes, the highest of which is the class of the Brahmins. Sometimes subdivisions are added as well as groups of people whose status is lower than any of the four regular classes. All these divisions have one thing in common: Brahmins are at the top; Brahmins are higher than other human beings. They owe this to their birth but also to the supernatural knowledge that they are deemed to possess. They use this knowledge in various ways, such as the performance of the rituals in which they are specialized and for which only they are qualified. In terms of knowledge, Brahmins expect nothing from anyone else.

In this situation, it is barely surprising that many Brahmins, especially the most traditional among them, had no sympathy for the new belief in rebirth and karmic retribution. Not only that, they ignored it to the extent possible. This attitude finds expression in the most traditional school of Brahmanical thought, Mimamsa, which specialized in the interpretation of Vedic texts and the performance of Vedic ritual. The classical text of this school—the commentary whose author was called Shabara—dates from the middle of the first millennium C.E., some nine centuries after the death of the Buddha (now usually dated around the year 400 B.C.E.). At that time the belief in rebirth and karmic retribution had been around for at least a millennium, perhaps longer. And yet, this Mimamsa text, though several thousand pages long and often dealing with the post-mortem consequences of rites, shows no interest whatsoever in this belief. We must assume that Shabara had heard of it but that, in true Brahmanical fashion, he ignored it.

Brahmanical Resistance

Interestingly, the belief in rebirth and karmic retribution appears to have become so widespread during the centuries surrounding the beginning of the Common Era that many Brahmins could not simply ignore it. Indeed, we have clear historical traces to show that certain Brahmins made a point of criticizing what was for them a new belief.

This Brahmanical resistance organized itself in the course of time and gave rise to a school of thought—called Lokayata or Carvaka—that flourished for a while and produced a number of texts. These texts are now lost because this Brahmanical school lost out in the long run against the belief in rebirth and karmic retribution, whose success on the Indian subcontinent became total. But this took time. We know that representatives of the Carvaka school of thought still existed toward the end of the first millennium C.E. After that date they disappeared, and their texts were no longer copied. Indeed, around the year 1000 the Persian traveler Alberuni could write: "As the word of confession 'There is no god but God, Muhammad is his prophet' is the shibboleth of Islam, the Trinity that of Christianity, and the institute of the Sabbath that of Judaism, so metempsychosis is the shibboleth of the Hindu religion. Therefore, he who does not believe in it does not belong to them and is not reckoned as one of them." Criticism of the Carvakas went on for quite a while, even after the year 1000 C.E., but they now were mere strawmen to whom one could attribute all imaginary forms of wickedness because there were no real Carvakas around any longer to defend themselves.

Absorption into Brahmanism

A third group of Brahmins felt attracted to the belief in rebirth and karmic retribution from an early date onward. They were, however, confronted with a dilemma. Accepting an outside belief was almost equivalent to admitting that the Brahmins were not the guardians of all spiritual knowledge and therefore to renouncing the special status that Brahmins claimed for themselves in society. Accepting rebirth and karmic retribution while yet remaining a Brahmin was only possible if it could be proved that this new belief was not new at all, that it was found in the Veda. This was not easy, but several texts of the period show that efforts were made to do so.

Perhaps the earliest Brahmanical texts that show awareness of rebirth and karmic retribution connect this belief with a form of secret knowledge that is presented in various Vedic texts, the "knowledge of the five fires." About this knowledge, the *Brihadaranyaka Upanishad* (6.2), presumably dating from the last two centuries B.C.E., states the following:

The people who know this and the people there in the wilderness who venerate truth as faith—they pass into the flame, from the flame into the day, from the day into the fortnight of the waxing moon, from the fortnight of the waxing moon into the six months when the sun moves north, from these months into the world of the gods, from the world of the gods into the sun, and from the sun into the region of lightning. A person consisting of mind comes to the regions of lightning and leads him to the worlds of Brahma. The exalted people live in those worlds of Brahma for the longest time. They do not return.

The people who win heavenly worlds, in contrast, by offering sacrifices, by giving gifts, and by performing austerities—they pass into the smoke, from the smoke into the night, from the night into the fortnight of the waning moon, from the fortnight of the waning moon into the six months when the sun moves south, from these months into the world of the fathers, and from the world of the fathers into the moon. Reaching the moon they become food. There, the gods feed on them, as they tell King Soma, the moon: "Increase! Decrease!" When that ends, they pass into this very sky, from the sky into the wind, from the wind into the rain, and from the rain into the earth. Reaching the earth, they become food. *They are again offered in the fire of man and then take birth in the fire of woman.* Rising up once again to the heavenly worlds, they circle around in the same way.

Those who do not know these two paths, however, become worms, insects, or snakes.

This passage describes some kind of cycle ("they circle around in the same way") but contains no hint of karmic retribution. What is more, only the sentence in italics clearly states that the passage concerns rebirth in this world, and this sentence is missing in one of the two versions of this Upanishad. In other words, if this passage is about rebirth and karmic retribution at all, it has left out karmic retribution and manages to be extremely unclear about rebirth. What is more, the notion that knowledge of the true inactive nature of the self may lead to the end of rebirths is totally absent.

What *is* present in this passage is the idea that people who possess some kind of knowledge "do not return." This is interesting and in a way not even surprising. The Brahmins considered themselves the guardians of higher knowledge, including the kind of knowledge one needs to reach high spiritual goals. Confronted with others who claimed that there was a kind of knowledge (knowledge of the inactive nature of the self) that led to a high spiritual goal (liberation from rebirth and karmic retribution), certain Brahmins borrowed part of the goal ("they do not return") and replaced the liberating knowledge with a form of Vedic knowledge. These Brahmins, to put it bluntly, had hardly or not at all understood the issues at stake, yet they claimed that spiritual knowledge could only be provided by them and their tradition.

A parallel passage occurs in another late-Vedic text, roughly dating from the same time, the *Chandogya Upanishad* (5.10):

> Now, the people who know this...they pass into the flame, from the flame into the day, from the day into the fortnight of the waxing moon, from the fortnight of the waxing moon into the six months when the sun moves north, from these months into the year, from the year into the sun, from the sun into the moon, and from the moon into lightning. Then a person who is not human— he leads them to Brahma. This is the path leading to the gods.
>
> The people here in villages, in contrast, who venerate thus— "Gift-giving is offerings to gods and to priests"—they pass into the smoke, from the smoke into the night, from the night into the fortnight of the waning moon, and from the fortnight of the waning moon into the six months when the sun moves south. These do not reach the year but from these months pass into the world of the fathers, and from the world of the fathers into space, and from space into the moon. This is King Soma, the food of the gods, and the gods eat it. They remain there as long as there is a residue, and then they return by the same path by which they arrived—first to space, and from space to the wind. After the wind has formed, it turns into smoke; after the smoke has formed, it turns into a thunder cloud; after the thunder cloud has formed, it turns into a rain cloud; and after the rain cloud has formed, it rains down. On earth they spring up as rice and barley, plants and trees, ses-

ame and beans, from which it is extremely difficult to get out. When someone eats that food and deposits the semen, from him one comes into being again.

Now, *people here whose behavior is pleasant can expect to enter a pleasant womb,* like that of a woman of the Brahmin, the Kshatriya, or the Vaishya class. But *people of foul behavior can expect to enter a foul womb,* like that of a dog, a pig, or an outcaste woman.

Then there are those proceeding on neither of these two paths—they become the tiny creatures that return many times. "Be born! Die!"—that is a third state.

This passage claims that the right Vedic knowledge leads to Brahma, to the gods. In light of the preceding passage, we may interpret this to mean that those who possess this knowledge "do not return." This remains, however, unsaid. Our passage is more outspoken with regard to rebirth and karmic retribution: "people here whose behavior is pleasant can expect to enter a pleasant womb,...people of foul behavior can expect to enter a foul womb." There can therefore be no doubt that we are here confronted with the belief in rebirth and karmic retribution, though dressed up in Vedic garb.

Both passages just considered are presented as the teaching of a king to a Brahmin. This is highly irregular. Normally Brahmins are the teachers, for Brahmins claim to possess spiritual knowledge. This irregularity did not escape the authors of these passages. They make the king state in so many words that before now—that is, before the events related—this knowledge was not available to Brahmins. One of the two passages adds that this lack of knowledge on the part of Brahmins that kings yet possessed was responsible for the fact that so far "government has belonged exclusively to royalty." This is to my knowledge the only explicit admission in Vedic texts that non-Brahmins were in the possession of knowledge that Brahmins did not have but were nevertheless interested in. It also constitutes proof that rebirth and karmic retribution were notions that were taken over from others by some Brahmins at that time. It is easy to guess who those others were: they were the people of the region and milieu to which Jainism, Buddhism, and the other currents discussed here belonged.

Our discussion so far shows that the first Brahmanical attempts to absorb the new ideas were clumsy. In the passages considered, only bits and pieces had been taken over and given a Brahmanical shape. The inner coherence of the ideas had largely escaped the attention of their authors. This changed subsequently. More recent passages from the *Brihadaranyaka Upanishad* repeatedly point out that "a man turns into something good by good action and into something bad by bad action." More to the point, we find here an understanding that knowledge of a self that is not affected by action is vital if one wishes to escape from karmic retribution:

> This immense, unborn self is none other than the one consisting of perception here among the vital functions. There, in that space within the heart, he lies—the controller of all, the lord of all, the ruler of all! *He does not become more by good actions or in any way less by bad actions....*
>
> About this self, one can only say "not—, not—." He is ungraspable, for he cannot be grasped. He is undecaying, for he is not subject to decay. He has nothing sticking to him, for nothing sticks to him. He is not bound; yet he neither trembles in fear nor suffers injury.
>
> These two thoughts do not pass across this self at all: "Therefore, I did something bad"; and "Therefore, I did something good." *This self, rather, passes across both of those thoughts; he is not burnt by anything that he has done or left undone.*

In other words, an understanding of the complex of ideas in which rebirth and karmic retribution have their place begins to find its way into at least some Brahmanical texts.

In the last passage considered, the notion of a self that is inactive and that remains unaffected by all does make an appearance, perhaps its first appearance in Brahmanical literature (though not in Indian literature in general). This is a notion that many Brahmins adopted with gusto. Indeed, we will see below that it became central in much of what we habitually refer to as Brahmanical philosophy. The attraction of this notion in late-Vedic times may have been increased by the fact that the Vedic tradition had, in its own right, become very interested in the self. In the properly Vedic context this interest in the self had nothing to do with liberation, freedom from action, and, ultimately, freedom from rebirth. The Vedic tradition, before it became infiltrated by the "foreign" ideas we have been considering, had other concerns. One of these had to do with the hidden relations that exist between things. It was believed that many apparently unrelated things are yet connected. The numerous "magical identifications" of late-Vedic literature are meant to bring these connections to light. The idea behind these hidden connections is that by influencing one of the related terms one may exert an influence on the other. These hidden connections are supposedly revealed by similarities, if ever so remote, between things, or even by similarities of the words used to designate them. The connected things often belong to different realms, primarily macrocosm and microcosm, that is, the cosmic realm and the personal realm. In this search for connections, Vedic thinkers had almost inevitably hit upon the ultimate macrocosmic entity, that which encompasses all, and had connected it with the innermost part of the human being. This led to the identification of Brahma with the self. This self, let me repeat it once again, was not the self knowledge of which was essential to attain liberation. Most important, it was not inactive. But once certain Brahmins became interested in the notion of liberation through knowledge of the truly inactive self, it was easy to identify the two. This is what happened, as we will see later on.

We have so far only spoken of the influence on Brahmanism of the belief in liberation through knowledge of the inactive self. However, this was only one of the ways in which liberation might be attained. We have considered Jainism as an example of an alternative method: through immobility asceticism. This method, too, found its way into Brahmanism. And here, too, an attempt was made to assimilate these new practices to practices that were already current in the Vedic tradition. The Vedic sacrifice, in some of its forms, required from its practitioners various kinds of abstentions: fasts, reduction of sleep, sexual abstinence, for example. These restrictions were in principle to be observed for the duration of the sacrifice; they concern the consecrated sacrificer. However, some Brahmins extended the state of consecration to the whole or a major part of their lives, living in this way ascetic lives.

The Vedic tradition was not unanimous regarding the desirability of extended Vedic asceticism. It clashed with a major concern of the Vedic tradition: the need to produce sons. Vedic asceticism is therefore criticized in the Vedic texts themselves, as in the following stanza in the *Aitareya Brahmana*:

> By means of a son have fathers always crossed over the deep darkness, since he was born as their self from their self. He is a ship provided with food, that carries over to the other shore.
>
> What is the use of dirt, what of an antelope skin? What is the use of a beard, what of asceticism? Wish for a son, O Brahmins....

Sons, it was believed, are somehow essential for the post-mortem well-being of their deceased ancestors. Ascetics who produce no sons imperil the well-being of their ancestors. The *Mahabharata* illustrates this with the tale of such an ascetic, Jaratkaru, whose total sexual abstinence has left him without a son. During his wanderings he comes across his ancestors, who find themselves in an extremely disagreeable position: they are suspended in a hole, heads down, attached to a rope that a rat is about to gnaw through. All this, it turns out, is the result of Jaratkaru's refusal to procreate.

It is clear, then, that Vedic Brahmanism had an ascetic tradition of its own, which may well have come about without external influence. When external influence did present itself, in the form of immobility asceticism, it could be hooked onto what was already there. The Vedic tradition could in this way absorb an external element while at the same time claiming to continue something of its own. The combination led to a peculiar succession of more or less ascetic stages of life.

The ideal life of a male high-class person came to be depicted as a succession of four such stages, the four so-called ashramas. At a young age already—the texts mention ages from around eight to twelve years—the boy is supposed to join the family of a teacher so as to become a religious student *(brahmacarin)*. There he will be subjected to strict discipline while studying his Veda, for a period of some twelve years. Having finished this first ashrama, he is ready to become a householder. In this stage he is expected to marry and produce sons. This period comes to an end when he sees his first grandchild or when he discovers his first grey hair; the texts are not unanimous about this. The householder now withdraws, with his wife and with his sacrificial fire, to a hut in the forest, where he lives off what the forest produces. He continues to perform his ritual obligations and dedicates himself to ascetic practices. He is now a *vanaprastha,* a "forest-dweller." This period, too, comes to an end, when the *vanaprastha* abandons all that remains to him—including his wife and his sacrificial fire—in order to become a *sannyasin,* a renouncer wandering from village to village, begging for his food. During this final stage he is expected to attain liberation from rebirth and karmic retribution.

It is quite clear that this succession of four ashramas is a theoretical construct that does not correspond to anything actually observed. Indeed, our oldest textual sources present these four ashramas not as succeeding stages, but as four options out of which the student who has mastered his Veda must choose one. He can remain a student and stay on in the family of his teacher and master further Vedas. He can also marry and create a family. Third, he can withdraw into the forest and live an ascetic life dedicated to the performance of rites. Or finally, he adopts the life of the religious mendicant, surviving by begging. Ashramas three and four, in particular, correspond to forms of religious life we have already encountered before. Ashrama three, that of the forest-dweller, corresponds to the life of the Vedic ascetic. Ashrama four, that of the renouncer, corresponds rather closely to the way of life and to the aims of the non-Brahmanical aspirants to liberation. The renouncer searches the true nature of his self, adopting the way of mendicancy that so many others, including the early Buddhists and Jainas, had adopted.

It can be seen that the way to liberation through knowledge of the inactive nature of the self has found its place in the scheme of the four ashramas, both in its earlier form in which they constitute four options and in the later form where they have become stages of life. The way to liberation through immobility asceticism is not so clearly included in the scheme: the asceticism of the third ashrama is primarily Vedic asceticism, related to the sacrificial life-style. This does not mean that immobility asceticism found no adherents in Brahmanical circles. Other early texts, among them the great Sanskrit epic called *Mahabharata,* speak a lot of ascetics who aspire to liberation through such asceticism. The term often used is Yoga. The yogi is depicted as stopping all or a selection of bodily and mental functions. Occasionally he is described as being as motionless as a log of wood or as a mountain. The suppression of breath in particular is a recurring theme in his practices. But there is a tendency to associate these forms of immobility asceticism with knowledge of the true nature of the self. This knowledge is called Sankhya. Yoga and Sankhya, a number of texts proclaim, go together; they are but two sides of the same spiritual practice. This shows that the two main solutions to the problem of rebirth and karmic retribution that we have come across—suppression of all activity on one hand, knowledge of the inactive nature of one's true self on the other—are here combined into one single spiritual path that covers both.

Why were there Brahmins with an interest in the (for them) new belief of rebirth and karmic retribution? It is possible that they were attracted to it for personal reasons. However, another facture is likely to have played a role, too. Brahmanism, initially centered in a region of northern India, subsequently spread over an ever larger area, until it covered most of the South Asian subcontinent and much of Southeast Asia as well. This spread took the form of Brahmins traveling into different regions, offering their services as specialists of the supernatural. What these Brahmins did not, or not primarily, try was converting the inhabitants of those regions to worshiping different gods or even to different forms of religious practice. As far as the worshiping of gods and religious practice were concerned, it was rather the Brahmins who had to be flexible. It is for this reason that we soon see Brahmins involved in forms of religion very hospitable to local cults and in forms of religious practice (such as temple cults) far removed from the ritual practices of Vedic religion. Only one element remains unchanged: the Brahmanical vision of a hierarchical society in which they, the Brahmins, occupied the highest position as exclusive guardians of the spiritual realm.

In this situation it will be clear that it was almost unavoidable that Brahmanism, in those regions where many local residents believed in rebirth and karmic retribution, was going to absorb this belief and would claim that this belief was and had always been part of the

Brahmanical tradition. The meeting between Brahmanism and other religious cults and traditions was not a theoretical confrontation between two or more different claims about the supernatural. Quite on the contrary, there was a lot of accommodating in the realm of the supernatural. If there was a confrontation, it concerned primarily the social world. Here the Brahmins claimed preeminence. We know that in the long run they attained their goal in most parts of South Asia (and for a while in certain parts of Southeast Asia), but in doing so they absorbed a number of the originally non-Brahmanical religious elements they came across.

One might think that the belief in rebirth and karmic retribution would suit Brahmanical ideology. Brahmins claimed preeminence in the world and the right to various favors and privileges. Would it not be tempting to maintain that they had acquired this preeminence and the accompanying rights on account of their good deeds in earlier lives? This would give a justification to a claim that not everyone might be inclined to accept.

There can be no doubt that this temptation was present. As a matter of fact, the passage of the *Chandogya Upanishad* considered above contains a line that proves this: "Now, people here whose behavior is pleasant can expect to enter a pleasant womb, like that of a woman of the Brahmin, the Kshatriya, or the Vaishya class." There are also numerous passages, already in Brahmanical texts like the *Mahabharata,* that predict rebirth as an outcaste for those who misbehave. This is not even surprising, for Buddhism, too, saw in karma the explanation of social status. And yet, Brahmins did not jump onto this as a justification for their claims of superiority. They had a mythological justification for this state of affairs, which is repeated over and over again in Brahmanical literature. It is part of an account of creation, in which the creator god used his own body to produce the different classes: the Brahmin from his mouth, the Kshatriya from his arms, the Vaishya from his thighs, the Shudra from his feet. This account has nothing to do with the belief in rebirth and karmic retribution: the classes owe their different positions to an event—perhaps one may say: decision—that took place in primeval times.

The *Laws of Manu,* a Brahmanical text dating perhaps from the third or fourth century C.E., illustrates this ambiguous attitude. This text knows the doctrine of rebirth and karmic retribution, and refers to it regularly, usually to threaten its users with the horrible consequences of illicit acts. It does not use this doctrine to justify the privileges that some (especially the Brahmins) feel entitled to, except in its final book, which may well be a later addition.

It is easy to make an informed guess as to the reasons why Brahmanism took time to adopt the notion that good deeds in earlier lives are the justification for the preeminence of Brahmins. This explanation, though convenient, starts from the assumption that there is a fundamental continuity between the different classes (and animal species for that matter). One's present position may be the result of deeds carried out in an earlier life, but one's present deeds may result in a much higher or lower position in a future life. A Brahmin and a Shudra in this life may exchange roles in a next one. It is clear that this kind of reasoning introduces a relativistic element into class distinctions and threatens to take away the absolute and fundamental distinction that Brahmins had claimed so far. Such an absolute and fundamental distinction is still postulated in the *Laws of Manu,* for example, in the following passage (Manu 1.28–30):

> As they are brought forth again and again, each creature follows on its own the very activity assigned to it in the beginning by the Lord. Violence or nonviolence, gentleness or cruelty, righteousness or unrighteousness, truthfulness or untruthfulness—whichever he assigned to each at the time of creation, it stuck automatically to that creature. As at the change of seasons each season automatically adopts its own distinctive marks, so do embodied beings adopt their own distinctive acts.

Seen this way, no Brahmin is in danger of being surpassed by someone of lower rank, not even in a future life. In spite of this obvious advantage, the belief in rebirth and karmic retribution succeeded in making itself ever more present in these discussions, so much so that karma is frequently invoked, even today, to justify the hierarchy of castes.

The conviction that Brahmins belong to an altogether different category from other human beings finds expression in the widely held belief (among Brahmins) that they constitute a separate spe-

cies *(jati)*. This is a point of view against which Buddhists have pro-
tested all along, presumably already in one of their canonical texts,
the *Sutta Nipata*. Some verses of this text (650–652) can be translated
as follows:

> One is not a Brahmin by species [*jati*]; one is not a non-Brahmin
> by species. One is a Brahmin on account of one's former deeds
> [*karma*]; one is a non-Brahmin on account of one's former deeds.
>   One is a farmer…a craftsman…a merchant…a servant…a
> thief…a warrior…a sacrificer…a king on account of one's for-
> mer deeds.

The verses are somewhat ambiguous, for *jati* can also mean "birth,"
and *karma* can also refer to present deeds. However, the use of these
alternative meanings gives a translation that is less satisfactory. In
the present interpretation, these verses deal with an issue that we also
meet with in the *Laws of Manu*, although this issue is dealt with from
two opposing points of view there.

Class, Species, and Universal in Indian Philosophy

Brahmins liked to think of themselves as a separate species, as
different from humans of lower rank as a cat is different from
a dog. This is hardly surprising, for it is difficult to think of a
better justification for the social status quo in which the Brahmins lived (or that they wished to impose) than the recognition
that this situation corresponds to the nature of things, just as
it corresponds to the nature of things that cats and dogs have
different habits and needs. It is probably a general rule that the
privileged layers of all societies look for justifications for the
status quo; racial (and racist) theories are often invoked elsewhere in the world to justify a skewed division of privileges
among people of different skin color.

Buddhists in India did not take long to accept the status
quo when the Brahmanical layering of society managed to impose itself: we know that there were a considerable number of
Buddhist Brahmins during the first millennium C.E., people
who had become Buddhists without abandoning their status as

Brahmins. However, Buddhism never accepted the theoretical justification that saw in Brahmins a separate species. Indeed, the message preached by Buddhism concerned all human beings, irrespective of their social status; with respect to the Buddhist road to liberation, all human beings were equal.

An ongoing debate about the equal or unequal status of human beings opposed Brahmanism and Buddhism for as long as they coexisted on the Indian subcontinent. Interestingly, this debate also came to cover a philosophical issue that, at first sight, has no connection whatsoever with questions concerning the organization of society. This philosophical issue is the putative existence of universals.

Universals, to put it briefly, are entities whose existence was postulated by certain Brahmanical thinkers to account for the fact that the objects of our experience usually appear in groups that have something in common. The word *vase,* for example, does not refer to just one object; it covers all vases. All these objects that we call vases must therefore have something in common that allows us to cover them all with the help of one single word. The "thing" they have in common is the universal that accompanies, or rather that inheres in, all vases. The Brahmanical thinkers concerned claimed that universals are existing things, so that a vase and its universal are two different things. Buddhist ontology (see the boxed text "Buddhist Scholasticism and the Beginning of Indian Philosophy") had no place for universals and rejected their existence.

One of the words that philosophers used for "universal" is *jati,* the same word that also means species. This should not surprise us, for clearly, if vases have a universal, cats will have one too, and so will dogs. Animal species are therefore a special instantiation of universals. Now Brahmins wished to be seen as a separate species, with the implication that Brahmins have a universal of their own. The Buddhists, from their side, refused to acknowledge that there are any universals at all, so for them the Brahmins did not have one either.

The adoption of rebirth and karmic retribution, then, posed challenges to the Brahmanical tradition. We have seen some of these and will see more as we proceed. Here it is time to consider an attempt (a successful one) made by Brahmins to turn this belief to their advantage, that is, to strengthen their vision of society with its help. The notion of liberation plays a central role in it, especially the conviction that knowledge of the inactive nature of the self is required to attain that goal. This particular application of the belief of rebirth and karmic retribution finds its most famous expression in the *Bhagavadgita,* which in part addresses the following questions.

The *Bhagavadgita*

The *Bhagavadgita* is part of the *Mahabharata,* the biggest of the two Sanskrit epics (the *Ramayana* is the name of the other one). Some scholars think that the *Bhagavadgita* is an insertion into the *Mahabharata.* Others believe they can identify insertions into the *Bhagavadgita* itself, but these issues are still hotly debated. But whether originally independent or otherwise, the *Bhagavadgita* has gained celebrity all of its own and is indeed one of the fundamental texts of Hinduism in many of its forms.

The text presents us with a discussion between a warrior, Arjuna, and his charioteer, Krishna. It becomes soon clear that Krishna is an incarnation (an *avatara*) of the supreme God Vishnu, but initially he is no more than a charioteer who listens to the complaints and concerns of Arjuna. The scene is situated just before the beginning of a major battle, in which two opposing armies are preparing themselves to destroy each other. Arjuna's difficulty is that there are many friends and relatives in the opposing army, and he wonders whether it would not be better to give up and withdraw from this for him repugnant situation and choose a simpler life. It is Krishna's elaborate response that has made the text famous. This response gives expression to the Brahmanical view in which everyone must carry out the tasks linked to his position in life. Since Arjuna is a warrior, he must fight and not give in to weakness. This relatively simple answer is subsequently elaborated and comes to cover far more than Arjuna alone or even warriors alone. An important element of Krishna's message is that everyone must carry out the tasks linked to his position in society but not in order to gain their fruits. Quite on the contrary, one must carry out these tasks in a disinterested manner. Elaborating further, Krishna admonishes Arjuna to dedicate the fruits of his actions to God, that is, to Krishna. It is in this part of the *Bhagavadgita* that we come across the notion of *bhakti* (devotion), a notion that gained enormously in importance in subsequent centuries (see below).

If our true self does not act, who then is responsible for the deeds that we yet appear to be carrying out? If it is not I who performs them, who does? Thinkers associated with Sankhya, which we met above, had an answer to this question that amounts to this: impersonal forces are at work to keep our material and mental parts going. These impersonal forces are emphatically different from the real self, but most people do not know this. They identify with actions for which, when it comes to it, they are not responsible. As a result they are the victims of rebirth and karmic retribution.

What happens once one realizes that one's deeds are in reality not one's own, that they are produced by forces that are different from one's true self? Here the *Bhagavadgita* offers the following answer: In that situation the impersonal forces will make a person act in accordance with his or her station in life. A warrior, if he is wise enough to understand how the world is constituted, will fight a battle, even if he has serious doubts about its desirability. This example, incidentally, is highly relevant in the context of the *Bhagavadgita*. This text initially describes the inner struggles of a mighty warrior, Arjuna, who would like to avoid his next battle. His charioteer Krishna, who is really an incarnation *(avatara)* of the highest God Vishnu, tells him that he should simply carry out his duties as a warrior, without regard for the results, for those are the tasks linked to his station in life.

It is interesting to recall at this point the strict determinism that we encountered in connection with Ajivikism. We found there that bodies were believed to act in accordance with impersonal karmic forces, obliging each individual to pass through a long series of births. The *Bhagavadgita,* though different in many respects from Ajivikism, agrees with it in stating that the body can act in accordance with impersonal forces, each one in agreement with its status in the world. In the case of the *Bhagavadgita,* this happens when its owner has realized his or her true identity. In Ajivikism there is no such requirement. The parallelism between the two is nevertheless striking and may not be due to mere coincidence.

The social consequences of the attitude preached in the *Bhagavadgita* are easy to fathom. It becomes a sign of spiritual advancement to acquiesce to the social position one is born in. It is even a condition for attaining liberation. Those who understand that not they themselves, but impersonal forces are responsible for their actions, will not obstruct those impersonal forces from doing their job. The result is behavior that agrees with one's position in life: a Brahmin will behave like a Brahmin, a Kshatriya like a Kshatriya, a Vaishya like a Vaishya, and a Shudra like a Shudra. No one will protest, and everyone will accept the social hierarchy without complaints. Ideas that were initially cultivated in circles that sought escape from society are in this manner turned into pillars of the kind of society Brahmins envisage.

To conclude this chapter, a few words must be said about the use to which the belief in rebirth and karmic retribution was put in the medieval (and numerous) Brahmanical texts known by the name Puranas. These texts often reserve a chapter for a discussion of the so-called ripening of karma *(karma-vipaka).* These chapters are usually placed in the context of the cosmological descriptions of hells and explain how people get there by committing sins. Tortures that fit the crime are depicted in great detail. However, these chapters are often followed by other ones on expiations, which supposedly interfere with the karmic machinery. In other words, the Puranas use karmic rhetoric (so to say), without abandoning older Vedic concepts that were believed to exert an influence on events.

CHAPTER 4

Karma and Philosophy

Accepting the belief in rebirth and karmic retribution is one thing. Understanding how and why it works is another. This problem confronted all of those who accepted this belief and particularly those who thought these topics were open to rational inquiry. This covered most of the intellectual elite of Jainism, Buddhism, and Brahmanism, especially from the early centuries C.E. onward. From that date onward a philosophical tradition established itself in the subcontinent, which developed systems of thought meant to explain the world we live in and in particular those aspects that concern us humans.

This philosophical tradition, in its various manifestations, also dealt with questions relating to rebirth and karmic retribution. Two questions in particular occupied the minds of the thinkers concerned. The first one was about liberation: how is liberation possible? By and large it can be said that most philosophical schools had this question at their core, for a very understandable reason. The attainment of liberation was most often thought of as accompanied by, or as depending upon, a special insight into the nature of the world and humanity's place in it. The philosophical systems of classical India present themselves frequently as being expressions of the insight required to attain liberation. They paid at least lip-service (sometimes more) to the idea that a thorough understanding of the respective philosophies was a precondition for liberation. The insight required differed from school to school, each one claiming that only they provided the knowledge without which liberation would remain out of reach.

The second question was more general. Besides an understanding of the solution (liberation from rebirth and karmic retribution), Indian philosophical thinkers were not completely uninterested in the problem: How does karmic retribution work in the case of those who are not close to and perhaps not even interested in liberation? What is the mechanism that is responsible for the fact that acts committed in this life will find retribution in a future one?

This problem has two sides. Both take for granted that deeds leave traces. These traces are most commonly assumed to remain attached to the person or to that part of the person that transmigrates from one life to the next. The first side of the problem needs, therefore, an answer in terms of what it is in the person that transmigrates and in what form the traces of acts carried out earlier move along with that person. This side of the problem is relatively straightforward.

There is another side to the problem. Even if one finds an answer to the question of how earlier actions leave traces that give rise to results in a future life, this does not yet answer the question of what mechanism guarantees that these results will be of a moral nature. What is it that makes good deeds have agreeable consequences and bad deeds, disagreeable ones? This question, once one thinks it through, reveals itself as being much more difficult to answer than one might be inclined to think at first sight. It is therefore not surprising that various texts state in so many words that karmic retribution is a problem that is beyond the intellectual capacities of human beings. The *Devibhagavata Purana* (6.10.34), a Brahmanical text of uncertain date, states, for example: "The course of karma in a breathing creature tied to a body is deep and mysterious, hard even for the gods to comprehend; so how could men understand it?" The *Mahabharata* (3.32.33) puts it this way: "The fruition of acts, both good and bad, their origin and disappearance, are the mysteries of the gods." The Buddha, too, according to the *Abhidharmakosha* of Vasubandhu, had said: "Karmic retribution of living beings is incomprehensible."

This second side of the problem, then, constituted a major challenge for Indian philosophical thinkers of the early Common Era, who were not yet ready to easily admit defeat. It raised the issue of teleology, of goal-directed mechanisms in and around the human being. The retribution of acts does not always correspond to the goals of the person who has carried them out (a bad person does not normally aspire to be punished), so that the question does not concern goal-directed behavior of human beings. Indeed, who would consciously look for the negative consequences that result from their bad deeds? Some other factors must be at work, which pursue goals (and attain them) that are not the goals of the person to which they redound.

The question of karmic teleology, which affected most schools of Indian philosophy, will be separately discussed later on. We will first consider the ways in which the main philosophical schools developed a picture of reality that allowed for the possibility of liberation and also specified the nature of the traces that deeds leave behind in a person, traces that give rise to results in a future life.

Buddhist Scholasticism and the Beginning of Indian Philosophy

Systematic philosophy in India begins within Buddhism, and more particularly within Buddhist scholasticism as it developed during the last centuries B.C.E. in the northwestern parts of the subcontinent. In order to understand why and how this happened, consider the following.

The third "basket" of the Buddhist canonical Tripitaka, the *Abhidharma-pitaka,* is dedicated to Abhidharma, "scholasticism." This part of the canon has in its entirety survived in two different versions: one belonging to the Theravada Buddhists (at present mainly found in Sri Lanka and several countries of Southeast Asia), the other to the Sarvastivada school of Buddhism. This latter school has disappeared, but many of its texts have survived, some in Sanskrit, many more in Chinese translation.

Buddhist Abhidharma is concerned with the preservation and analysis of the teaching of the Buddha. Unlike the *Sutra-pitaka,* which preserves the sermons of the Buddha as they were believed to have been uttered by him, in Abhidharma key concepts (called *dharmas*) occurring in those sermons are enumerated, classified, and related to each other. This is done in considerable detail, with the result that many Abhidharma

texts are tedious reading. In some cases, however, this tedious-
ness hides important theoretical developments that signal the
beginning of systematic philosophy in India. This is especially
true of the scholastic texts of the Sarvastivadins.

As a matter of fact, there is an important difference between
the contents of the *Abhidharma-pitaka* of the Theravadins and
that of the Sarvastivadins. The texts contained in the latter
show a feature that is absent from the former: the attempt to
interpret the lists of *dharma*s in a manner that creates a coherent ontology, that is, a vision of what entities exist and how they
interact to give rise to the world familiar to us.

In brief, this was done as follows. The *dharma*s came to be
looked upon as existing entities and as the ultimate constituents of all that exists. A human being, for example, can be
thought of as a vast collection of physical and mental constituents: the surviving lists of *dharma*s were interpreted to fit this
role. Nonhuman sentient beings were also thought of in this
manner. Nonsentient objects were thought of as constituted of
physical *dharma*s only. The Sarvastivadins developed in this
way an atomic understanding of all that exists, where "atomic"
is to be understood in more than a mere physical sense: the
majority of constituent *dharma*s were of a mental nature. This
atomic vision of reality was given a temporal extension: the
*dharma*s were believed to be momentary, lasting but one moment. Sentient and insentient beings thus came to be looked
upon as vast collections of *dharma*s that, each of them, disappear as soon as they have come into being.

A further claim was added to the ontology just described. It
was maintained that only ultimate constituents have real existence; the things whose constituents they are do not really exist. This radical claim reduced the objects of our experience to
naught at one fell swoop. Buddhist texts explain that there is no
forest apart from the trees, no chariot apart from the wheels,
axles, and whatever else constitute it, and as a result no person,
or indeed anything else, apart from the *dharma*s.

This radical way of interpreting reality (which the Sarvastivadins believed was based on the words of the Buddha, even

though nothing is less true from the point of view of sober historical research) could not but raise numerous questions, and Buddhist scholiasts made a determined effort to answer them. One question was particularly urgent: if the world does not really consist of persons and ordinary objects such as houses and chariots, how is it that we all believe in their existence? The answer provided was as follows: We are misled by the words of language. We think there is a chariot because we have the word *chariot;* we think that there are persons (and that we ourselves are persons) because of words such as *person, I,* and so forth.

The ideas developed in the Sarvastivada school of thought exerted in subsequent centuries a profound influence on other schools of thought, including non-Buddhist schools (see the boxed texts titled "Vaisheshika as a Response to Sarvastivada" and "Shared Problems in Indian Philosophy"). One of its doctrines, however, was not taken over by others, even though it was considered important enough to give the school its name. *Sarvasti* in Sarvastivada consists of two parts, *sarva* and *asti,* which mean "all" and "exists" respectively. Together they refer to the doctrine according to which everything—present, past, and future things—exists. The school had indeed come to the conclusion that past and future things exist in a certain way. This at first sight bizarre position allowed them to solve a scholastic problem that it is not necessary to discuss here. However, once in place, it came in handy to solve other problems that the school was confronted with in later centuries. An example will be discussed in the main text, below.

There had been no systematic attempts at philosophizing in Buddhism (and in India in general) until the developments in Sarvastivada just described. This raises the question of why these developments took place. If an answer to this question can be found at all, it will have to take into consideration where and when they took place: in northwestern India, probably from the second century B.C.E. on. This area, during that period, had a strong Hellenistic cultural and political presence. As a matter of fact, the Greek successors of Alexander of Macedonia (Alexander the Great) ruled in this corner of the

subcontinent until about 150 B.C.E., and their cultural presence remained noticeable for several centuries after that. The
Greeks had a strong tradition of debate, and it seems likely that
the Buddhist missionaries who settled in that region were more
or less obliged to engage in debate with their potential converts. This in its turn obliged them to present to their interloc-
utors a consistent and coherent vision of the world, a vision of a
kind Buddhism had not possessed until that time.

Karma and Buddhist Philosophy

The acceptance of rebirth and karmic retribution is in India virtually inseparable from the conviction that there is a way to end it.
That is to say, most of our sources belong to currents or movements
that claim to know a method to stop rebirth and karmic retribution once and for all. These sources were primarily interested in issues connected with the solutions they offered and only secondarily
in the functioning of karmic retribution itself. Many Brahmins, for
example, had been taken in by the idea that knowledge of the unchanging and inactive nature of the self was an essential ingredient
of the path to liberation. Unsurprisingly, many of the Brahmanical
philosophical systems are intrigued by the question how human beings, who live and act in the world, can have a core—their deepest
self or soul—that does not act at all. We will learn more about these
systems in the next section. Here we will concentrate on Buddhist
philosophy.

Knowledge of the self played no role in the Buddhist path to liberation. Many Buddhists went one step further and claimed that there
is no self, that there is no enduring core that transmigrates from one
body to another. This belief gained in significance against the background of another belief that came to prevail in Buddhism, the belief that all existing things are momentary. A living being, seen this
way, is a collection of momentary entities, and there is nothing in
this living being that survives for longer than a single moment. It
will be clear that, against the background of such a philosophy, the
very notion of transmigration becomes problematic. What is it that
transmigrates, if there is nothing that lasts longer than a moment? If

we must conclude from this that there is nothing that transmigrates, how then can we conceive of transmigration? And indeed, if there is nothing in a person that lasts longer than a single moment, how can we speak and think of a single person at all? If "I" am no more than a stream of momentary entities, so are "you." How then is it possible to keep the two streams of momentary entities—"my" stream and "your" stream—apart?

Buddhist thinkers soon realized that these questions can be answered on condition that the different streams of momentary entities be continuous. Just as we can keep two rivers apart because the constituent water particles of one river constitute one continuous stream that is different from the other stream, so the constituent momentary entities that belong to one person can be kept apart from those that belong to someone else.

This comparison helps, but only up to a point. The water particles of a river are not momentary, whereas the constituent entities of a person (and of everything else for that matter) are. These constituent entities were, confusingly, called *dharma*s. The terminology is confusing, for these *dharma*s have nothing whatsoever to do with merit, which too is called *dharma*. The Buddhist entities called *dharma*s, then, were momentary but yet formed continuous chains with other *dharma*s that preceded and succeeded them. This was possible because *dharma*s follow a strict causal law. As a matter of fact, the ancient Buddhist tradition had preserved a causal law called "dependent origination." The precise interpretation of this law was obscure even in the early days, but this law of dependent origination was believed to bring order in the chains of succeeding momentary *dharma*s. The resulting regularity is responsible for the fact that there is order in the world as we know it, that there are persons and objects that persist in time (at least for a while) even though they are in the end no more than collections of momentary entities.

The question of the continuity of the human person finds expression in an early text, the *Questions of King Milinda*, in which a Buddhist monk named Nagasena conducts a discussion with King Milinda; Milinda is the Indianized name of Menander, a Greek king who ruled in northwestern India in the second century B.C.E. In the midst of this long discussion the following passage occurs:

The king said: "He who is born, Nagasena, does he remain the same or become another?"

"Neither the same nor another."

"Give me an illustration."

"Now what do you think, O king? You were once a baby, a tender thing, and small in size, lying flat on your back. Was that the same as you who are now grown up?"

"No, that child was one; I am another."

"If you are not that child, it will follow that you have had neither mother nor father—no!—nor teacher. You cannot have been taught either learning, or behavior, or wisdom. Great king! Is the mother of the embryo in the first stage different from the mother of the embryo in the second stage, or the third, or the fourth? Is the mother of the baby a different person from the mother of the grown-up man? Is the person who goes to school one, and the same when he has finished his schooling another? Is it one who commits a crime, another who is punished by having his hands or feet cut off?"

"Certainly not. But what would you, Sir, say to that?"

The elder replied: "I should say that I am the same person, now I am grown up, as I was when I was a tender tiny baby, flat on my back. For all these states are included in one by means of this body."

"Give me an illustration."

"Suppose a man, O king, were to light a lamp. Would it burn the night through?"

"Yes, it might do so."

"Now, is it the same flame that burns in the first watch of the night, Sir, and in the second?"

"No."

"Or the same that burns in the second watch and in the third?"

"No."

"Then is there one lamp in the first watch, and another in the second, and another in the third?"

"No. The light comes from the same lamp all the night through."

"Just so, O king, is the continuity of a person or thing maintained. One comes into being, another passes away; and the rebirth is, as it were, simultaneous. Thus neither as the same nor as another does a man go on to the last phase of his self-consciousness."

Continuity is also the factor that links one existence to another one. The person reborn is a continuation of the one that died. The part of the person that continues into a next existence is referred to as name-and-form in the following passage, also from the *Questions of King Milinda:*

The king said: "What is it, Nagasena, that is reborn?"

"Name-and-form is reborn."

"What, is it this same name-and-form that is reborn?"

"No, but by this name-and-form deeds are done, good or evil, and by these deeds [this karma] another name-and-form is reborn."

"If that be so, Sir, would not the new being be released from its evil karma?"

The elder replied: "Yes, if it were not reborn. But just because it is reborn, O king, it is therefore not released from its evil karma."

"Give me an illustration."

"Suppose, O king, some man were to steal a mango from another man, and the owner of the mango were to seize him and bring him before the king and charge him with the crime. And the thief were to say: 'Your Majesty! I have not taken away this man's mangoes. Those that he put in the ground are different from the ones I took. I do not deserve to be punished.' How then would he be guilty?"

"Certainly, Sir. He would deserve to be punished."

"But on what ground?"

"Because, in spite of whatever he may say, he would be guilty in respect of the last mango that resulted from the first one [the owner set in the ground]."

"Just so, great king, deeds good or evil are done by this name-and-form and another is reborn. But that other is not thereby released from its deeds [its karma]."

Scholastic Buddhism made a major effort to enumerate the *dharma*s exhaustively and to analyze their functions, so much so that some of its early texts make us almost suspect that their authors had forgotten what had been the purpose of the teaching of the Buddha: to show the way to liberation from suffering and rebirth. This purpose manifests itself again in slightly younger scholastic texts, and one facilitating factor was the belief that the knowledge of all the *dharma*s was a precondition for enlightenment and liberation. This raised the further question of how and why such knowledge could have such an effect. Theories of great complexity were developed to answer this question, theories whose discussion at this place would take us too far afield.

Note by way of conclusion that scholastic Buddhism differentiated between various kinds of karma. Only some examples can be given here. Vasubandhu's *Abhidharmakosha Bhashya* (fourth or fifth century C.E.) distinguishes four kinds: (1) karma that is black, with black result; (2) karma that is white, with white result; (3) karma that is black-white, with black-white result; and (4) karma that is neither black nor white, with no result. The fourth type of karma leads to the destruction of karma. Vasubandhu justifies these categories by citing a canonical passage, and indeed the same idea can already be found in canonical texts. The *Visuddhimagga* of Buddhaghosa introduces no fewer than three fourfold divisions, the first one being (1) karma bearing fruit during the present lifetime, (2) karma bearing fruit in the next life, (3) karma bearing fruit in later lives, (4) karma that bears no fruit at all. Also the possible destinies one might reach after death were enumerated. The following categorization was widely accepted. Sentient beings can be reborn in five realms of existence: (1) hell, (2) the realm of animals; (3) the world of the shades, (4) human existence, and (5) existence as a god in heaven.

Karma and the Brahmanical Philosophies

We have already come across theoretical notions, accepted by some Brahmins, that were supposedly helpful or even necessary to bring about release from karmic retribution. They went by the name Sankhya, which presented itself as the theoretical counterpart of Yoga. In brief, Yoga preached liberation by way of immobility asceticism, and Sankhya did so through insight into the true inactive nature of the self. Sankhya attempted to clarify how an inactive self can yet be involved in an active world. Central to its explanation is the doctrine that besides an inactive self there are impersonal forces that are responsible for our deeds. In other words, the world consists of two different kinds of "things": on the one hand there are the inactive selves (one for each living being); on the other everything that is or can be active, which covers both the material and the mental world.

Note that the very problem that Sankhya attempts to solve obliges it to divide the world into two categories, which are not, as we might expect, the spiritual (or mental) and the material, but rather the inactive and the active. Everything we call mental and most of what we call spiritual belongs on the active side of this equation, as does the material world. All this activity, whether mental or material, is due to impersonal forces. On the inactive side there are only selves. Sankhya in its classical shape recognizes a plurality of selves, one for each living being.

It will be clear that there is relatively little one can say about the selves, given that they are completely inactive. As a matter of fact, Sankhya maintains that each self is conscious. Once again, we have to be careful not to misinterpret this in the light of modern concepts. The fact that each self is conscious does not imply that the self can think, for thinking is an activity. Consciousness, in order to obey the basic rules of the system, has to be inactive, motionless, unchanging. It is tempting to read in the notion of motionless consciousness a confirmation of the close links between Sankhya and Yoga, mentioned above. One might think that motionless consciousness is what yogis experience in their meditations. This, however, would be incautious. Our early sources, to begin with, do not suggest that the yogis of that time made efforts to attain states of motionless consciousness, but rather that they strove to attain unconsciousness. Second, given the fundamental assumptions and aims of Sankhya, there was only place for a motionless self. If that self was conscious, or consciousness, then that consciousness had to be motionless, too. There was, so to say, systemic pressure to think of consciousness in this manner.

Much more can be said about the active part of the world. Indeed, the Sankhya philosophy maintains that it consists of various constituents that arise out of an eternal substrate, Original Nature *(prakriti/ pradhana)*. The elements arise first out of Original Nature, then out of each other in a regular sequence that is believed to correspond to the re-creation of the world at the beginning of each cosmic cycle. Most important for our present purposes is that during this cosmic evolution entities appear that are capable of reflecting the consciousness of the selves. In this manner combinations arise of a conscious self, on the one hand, and physically and mentally active parts, on the other. These combinations correspond to what we would naively look upon as human (or other sentient) beings. Thus consciousness and activity (both physical and mental activity) seem to be inextricably interwoven, where in reality the two are distinct. Insight into this underlying reality permits persons to disentangle themselves from the knot, to become aware of their fundamentally inactive nature and of their noninvolvement in karmic retribution. Knowledge of this kind paves the way for liberation.

Another prominent Brahmanical school of thought (called Vaisheshika) elaborated a more sophisticated scheme. It looked upon the world as consisting essentially of substances, qualities, and actions. This accounts well for ordinary statements like "the blue vase stands on the table." Here the vase and the table are substances, the color blue is a quality that resides in the vase, and standing is the activity of the vase. This scheme was extended so as to cover less usual situations and things. The innermost self, for example, was categorized as an omnipresent and eternal substance. Following a widely held Indian belief, omnipresent things cannot move, and since Vaisheshika thought of movement as the quintessential form of activity, they cannot act either. This interpretation came in handy, for it was now necessary to think of the self as incapable of all action, precisely the outcome the Vaisheshika was looking for. However, being a substance, the self had to be endowed with qualities, just as more ordinary substances (such as vases) have qualities (such as color). For the self a special set of qualities had to be invented, and this is what the Vaisheshika school did. They introduced a number of qualities that can only reside in selves and nowhere else. Interestingly, they included consciousness in this list, thus coming up with a notion of consciousness (as a quality of the self) that is altogether different from the one we find in other schools of Indian philosophy. Since for the Vaisheshika consciousness is not identical with the self, but is a "mere" quality of it, it was not obliged to postulate that consciousness, like the self, had to be unchanging and motionless. This had been the position of the Sankhya school, for straightforward systemic reasons: for them the self was no different from consciousness and could therefore not be allowed to act. In Vaisheshika the situation was altogether different. The self is without activity, to be sure, but consciousness, a separable quality of the self, is not. The implications of this particular position are far-reaching. It means that conscious processes such as thought can and do take place, but, being qualities, they are not identical with the self. Worse, the self on its own is without qualities, and therefore not only omnipresent and eternal, but also unconscious. The liberated person, who has succeeded in freeing his or her self from all qualities, is therefore unconscious, too.

Vaisheshika as a Response to Sarvastivada

Vaisheshika ontology is best understood as a reaction to Sarvastivada ontology. Recall that Sarvastivada ontology comprised an exhaustive list of all there is (the *dharma*s), that it did not recognize the existence of composite objects (such as chariots and persons), but that it explained our belief in the existence of such objects with the help of the words of language (the word *chariot* makes us believe that there are chariots in the world). Vaisheshika, a Brahmanical philosophy, had no truck with Buddhist Sarvastivada and differed from the latter wherever it could. So where Sarvastivada accepted the list of *dharma*s (believed to have been pronounced by the Buddha) as the list of all there is, Vaisheshika created an altogether different list. Where Sarvastivada did not recognize the existence of composite objects, Vaisheshika emphatically did, maintaining, for example, that there is a chariot apart from, and different from, its constituent parts. And where Sarvastivada held that the words of language deceive us into thinking that the objects corresponding to words (such as chariots) exist, Vaisheshika claimed that words correspond to real objects. Interestingly, by trying in this way to distinguish itself in all details from Sarvastivada, Vaisheshika ended up with an ontology whose structure had much in common with the former: both had an exhaustive list of all that exists, both claimed that the world of our experience corresponds to the words of language, while their position with regard to composite entities represented two opposite extremes (according to Sarvastivada, chariots and other composite things do not exist; according to Vaisheshika, they exist and are altogether different from their constituent parts). Vaisheshika also imitated Sarvastivada in adopting a fundamentally atomic vision of matter and of time.

The way in which Vaisheshika construed its list of all there is had to be different from Sarvastivada and was influenced or even determined by its belief that words and things correspond to each other. Vaisheshika had learned from the Sanskrit grammarians that the main types of words are three in number: nouns, verbs, and adjectives. They concluded from this that the "things" in the world fall primarily into three categories: substances, actions, and qualities. To these three fundamental categories they added a few more. Their assumption that composite things are different from their constituent parts obliged them to accept that an object—say, a vase—and its two halves together constitute three different things. This required an answer to the question of what relation connects a vase with one of its own halves. They came up with "inherence," a relation that proved useful in other contexts, too: it connects "things" that cannot be separated from each other. A quality (say, a color) is connected with its substance (e.g., a table) by this same inherence, as is an action (say, the movement of a chariot) with its substance (the chariot). It is impossible to remove a vase from one of its halves, a color from the object it gives color to, an action from the substance that is in motion. Another addition to the list was the universal, which is present—once again through inherence—in all the individuals covered by the same word: vases have a universal, as do cats, dogs, and Brahmins (see the boxed text titled "Class, Species, and Universal in Indian Philosophy").

The total number of fundamental categories differed somewhat from author to author; six is the number proposed by a number of them, but some came up with additional categories and therefore with higher numbers.

Once the list of fundamental categories was in place, everything had to find a place in this scheme. The self, for example, could not be an action or a quality (or any of the added categories), so it had to be a substance. Like other substances, it can have qualities, even though these qualities are altogether different from the ones commonly found in other substances (such as color). One of these qualities is knowledge or consciousness. Action, however, cannot inhere in the self because an omnipresent substance cannot move. This suited Vaisheshika very well, given that knowledge of the self and of its inactive nature was a precondition for liberation from karmic retribution.

Some further details of the Vaisheshika philosophy will be presented below. Here it must suffice to note that it presents a picture of the world, to be sure, but also a scheme regarding how insight of this nature can help a person to end the qualities of the self and end up with a self free from all qualities and therefore unchanging, eternal, and free from rebirth and karmic retribution. A consequence of this particular understanding is that the liberated self is unconscious. It follows that liberation, for the adherents of this school, amounts to an eternal state devoid of all consciousness. The liberated person, as some texts put it, is "like a stone."

Other solutions to the question of how one's innermost self can be inactive were proposed, too. A solution that joined the philosophical debate relatively late (in the second half of the first millennium C.E.) but that subsequently gained wide popularity is the one proposed by the school called Advaita Vedanta. It emphasizes that the self of our ordinary experience is not our real innermost self because there is here an admixture of other elements. Our real self is identical with what is called Brahma, the highest principle behind the world of our experience. Brahma, as a matter of fact, is pure inactive consciousness. The realization that our innermost self is identical with Brahma frees us therefore from karmic consequences.

Advaita Vedanta goes further. Since Brahma is the highest principle behind the world of our experience, and since Brahma is inactive, the ceaseless activity of the common-sense world might be thought to pose a problem. The answer provided is that our common-sense world is illusory and does not really exist. This is a radical position to take and one that may not initially have found much sympathy in Brahmanical circles, which had so far emphasized the reality of the ordinary world and had accused the Buddhists of rejecting this reality. Shankara, one of the early philosophical thinkers of Advaita Vedanta, therefore met with opposition from within Brahmanism. Some other Brahmins did not hesitate to call him a crypto-Buddhist. In spite of this opposition the Advaita Vedanta of Shankara and his disciples has become extremely popular in India until this day.

The Sankhya philosophy was well aware that our material bodies do not survive death and that rebirth implies the formation of a new body. The consequence of this observation is that traces of past deeds cannot be carried over to a next life by the material body. The self, being pure consciousness and unchangeable, cannot fulfill this task either. Most of the thinkers of this school therefore felt compelled to postulate the existence of something different from both the self and the material body. They called it the subtle body. Every sentient being—perhaps better: every self—was believed to possess such a subtle body, which, unlike the material body, would not come to an end at death and transmigrate into a next existence. Indeed, one subtle body accompanies every self from the creation of the world until its dissolution, that is, during a full cosmic period. The subtle body has mental parts, and it is in these mental parts that the dispositions that will account for future births and karmic retribution have their place. This subtle body carries the "dispositions" that are responsible for the kind of rebirth one can expect in future lives. These dispositions are enumerated as falling in eight different categories: merit *(dharma)* and demerit *(adharma),* knowledge and ignorance, detachment and absence of detachment, power and absence of power. Each time the first item of these four pairs has a positive effect in a future life, the second a negative one. An exception has to be made for knowledge of the true nature of the self, which leads to liberation.

The Sankhya explanation of karmic retribution with the help of dispositions that were thought of as being instrumental in bringing about karmic consequences raised problems of its own. These dispositions were necessarily thought of as modifications of Original Nature. This confronted the Sankhyas with some serious difficulties, for Original Nature is completely resolved in its primordial state after the dissolution of one world period and before the beginning of a next one. No karmic traces would be able to survive in such a dissolved state. This was considered problematic. It would mean that, to take an extreme case, a person liberated in one world period would have to start all over again in the next one. This went against the most fundamental convictions of Sankhyas and non-Sankhyas alike. Various ways were explored to avoid this conclusion, but it was not easy to find a satisfactory answer. One Sankhya thinker went to the extent of denying the periodic destruction and re-creation of the world altogether, but this was such a dramatic proposal that it earned him the nickname "destroyer of Sankhya." The issue remained a source of embarrassment for the school and a cause of internal disagreement.

The Vaisheshika philosophy thought of the human self as a substance that can but does not have to be accompanied by certain qualities. The self being a special kind of substance, the qualities that inhere in it are special, too. We have already discussed consciousness: not the kind of immobile consciousness of Sankhya, but active consciousness with content, knowledge. However, there are also other qualities that only inhere in the self. There is a whole series of them, which together constitute the elements of a psychological theory. Let me explain.

The main qualities inhering in the self are knowledge *(buddhi)*, pleasure *(sukha)*, pain *(duhkha)*, desire *(iccha)*, repulsion *(dvesha)*, effort *(prayatna)*, merit *(dharma)*, demerit *(adharma)*, and subliminal impressions *(samskara)*. The order of this enumeration is not arbitrary. Knowledge of an object—usually perception—precedes the experience of pleasure or pain connected with it; this in its turn gives rise to desire and repulsion respectively; next in line comes effort that respectively seeks to obtain an object that is associated with desire and to avoid an object that is associated with repulsion; as a result merit and demerit come into being as well as subliminal impressions.

We see that the Vaisheshika scheme to explain human behavior has a behaviorist flavor about it, although it does not avoid terms relating to "inner" experiences. Behavior that leads to good experiences is repeated; behavior that leads to bad experiences is henceforth avoided. Desire and repulsion accompany conditioned behavior and cause repetition or avoidance of repetition of earlier behavior.

This is not the place to enter into a detailed discussion of the different qualities that inhere in the self. It is of importance to notice that the whole process here described takes place in—or perhaps one should say, *on*—the self. The process is an interplay of qualities of the self, most of which are quite independent of physical behavior. The one exception is effort *(prayatna)*. This quality of the self also constitutes a bridge with physical reality: when one makes an effort to do something, the physical body reacts and carries out the intended deeds. These deeds in their turn have an effect on the self: if one carries out good deeds, the quality merit *(dharma)* appears in the self; if one carries out bad deeds, the quality demerit *(adharma)* appears. With these two one is back in the self, and that is not yet the end of the story, for the qualities merit and demerit leave their traces in the form of another quality of the self, subliminal impressions *(samskara)*. These subliminal impressions are responsible for the karmic retribution that will take place, most commonly in a future existence.

It is possible to remove all qualities from the self. This requires prolonged and intense exertion and leaves, if successful, the self devoid of all these qualities and therefore without consciousness, "like a stone." Given the nature of the qualities of the self and their joint participation in the constitution of a psychological vision of the human being, it becomes clear what kind of exertion is required. It starts with the right knowledge, based on experience, that the pursuit of pleasure and the avoidance of pain is in the end not successful: suffering predominates as long as one remains involved in the psychological mechanism incorporated in the qualities of the self. Only an understanding that all this leads nowhere permits a person to put a stop to his or her involvement, to avoid desire and revulsion resulting from pleasure and pain, and to abstain from the effort that is meant to increase pleasure and reduce pain but in reality creates the merit and demerit that lead to karmic retribution. Full understanding (which includes understanding of the Vaisheshika system) is essential and will create in the person concerned detachment and the tendency to abstain from further activities.

The Theoretical Appropriation of Karma in Jainism

Details of the intellectual side of early Jainism are hard to come by. Its canon of holy scripture—supposedly containing the words of its most recent perfected teacher, Mahavira, a contemporary of the Buddha—is clearly a collection of in the main much more recent texts. According to the tradition of Jainas that accept this canon, the Shvetambaras, it was not collected until the fifth century C.E.; the other surviving Jaina tradition, that of the Digambaras, does not accept that it contains the words of Mahavira. This means that it is difficult to say anything certain about the way early Jainism conceived of karma. It is clear, however, that Jainism soon came to think of karma in "material" terms. Karma is thought of as a physical substance that clings to what we may call the soul *(jiva)* as dust clings to a wet cloth. Activity and certain mental weaknesses (false belief, lack of discipline, carelessness, the passions, and mental, physical and verbal activities) bring it about that karmic particles adhere to the soul. They accompany it when the soul travels from one existence into another. Suppression of activity and of those mental weaknesses removes the "stickiness" of the soul so that karma can no longer enter into contact with it. This is therefore a path of purification.

It is to be noted that Jainism, at least in its classical form, puts little or no emphasis on knowledge of the self as a liberating factor. These Jainas visualized the situation in terms of a number of fundamental entities—among those the soul and karma—whose interaction is responsible for continued existence and liberation. This different understanding of the world and of the mechanism of liberation in particular cannot be separated from the emphasis on asceticism in Jainism. Knowledge of the inactive nature of the self, for those who believed in it, was an essential condition for attaining liberation following a path that was at least in part cognitive/intellectual in character. Jainism has not always been insensitive to the attractions of this elegant way of attaining liberation, but for most of its history it opted for a more purely ascetic path. And here the "material" way of thinking of the elements involved proved satisfactory. In fact, the habit of thinking of karma in terms of material particles is no doubt responsible for the fact that Jainism developed a very rich literature on karma, in which numerous types and subtypes of karma were distinguished and minutely analyzed.

Fundamental to these analyses is the division of karma into eight categories, which are responsible for a variety of shortcomings and fulfill some other tasks, such as determining one's duration of life. The dustlike character of karma is particularly clear in its capacity to act like a screen that covers the omniscience that is yet the innate characteristic of each soul. Karma hides reality in this manner and confuses the individual souls. Only the removal off all karma returns omniscience to the soul and leads it to the state of liberation.

A point that merits attention is that the different way in which the Jainas visualized the world and the soul in particular permitted them to think of the soul as being coextensive with the body in which it finds itself. This does not mean that the soul always has the same size. As a matter of fact, its size varies in accordance with the size of the body in which it is reborn. The comparison is sometimes made with the light of a lamp that expands or contracts according to the size of the room in which it finds itself. In the same way the soul of a tiny insect and that of an elephant have the same size because the soul expands and contracts according to the body in which it is reborn.

But whatever the precise size of the Jaina soul, it is clear that it moves along with the body to which it belongs. In other words, some kind of activity can reasonably be ascribed to it. This would be a major difficulty if the Jainas were to believe that it is knowledge of the inactive nature of the self that is required for liberation. Such knowledge is not, however, part of the liberation requirements of most Jainas. This is no doubt one important reason why they could develop an altogether different understanding of the nature of karma. Karma being essentially a substance, it acquires in Jainism a sense that is rather far removed from its literal meaning of activity, movement. It is true that earliest Jainism may have thought of the soul in terms that were not all that different from those who believed that knowledge of the true inactive nature of the self was essential. It is also true that this notion exerted an attraction on certain more recent Jaina thinkers, among them the famous Kundakunda. But this notion remained relatively marginal to Jainism as a whole.

A few words must be said about the living being in which a soul might be reborn. This is a topic about which different thinkers did not always see eye to eye. From among plants and animals, Buddhism tended to consider only the latter potential destinies of transmigration (even though it was not always consistent in this limitation). The Brahmanical tradition, as so often, was not altogether uniform but did often include plants in the list of bodies in which one might be reborn. The Jainas' list was most comprehensive: it included even the elements, so that it recognized earth-, air-, water-, and fire-bodies, beside plants and the higher animals, gods, inhabitants of hell, and so forth. The chance of finding one's way up in subsequent births for souls that are embodied in, say, the elements must be considered vanishingly small. Indeed, Jainism considers that certain creatures (or rather the souls inhabiting them) are forever excluded from reaching liberation.

Theoretical Difficulties and Their Solutions

The problem discussed in this chapter and alluded to in an earlier chapter can be formulated most simply with the help of the following questions: How are karmic accounts kept? How is it that an impersonal force can function in such a manner that karmic retribution will be in accordance with the deeds performed? By what mechanism can a bad deed be punished in a future life and a good deed rewarded? If karmic retribution was thought of in terms of divine retribution, we might find the difficulty less daunting. But the belief in karmic retribution was often adhered to by people who did not accept the existence of a supreme god. In other words, there was no one to steer the process. Quite on the contrary, very often the gods themselves were believed to be subject to this mechanism of karmic retribution, in the face of which they, too, were helpless.

The difficulty is even more perplexing than it may appear at first sight. Karmic retribution does not only work for me or for you, but for everyone at the same time. The result is that numerous karmic strands are present simultaneously and must bring about results that are appropriate to all the agents involved. Suppose that two cars col-

lide and that the two drivers die in this accident. Two karmic strands
are supposedly at work here to bring about this result. One of the
two strands might have attained its goal equally well by directing its
driver to collide with, say, a tree; how did it "know" that the other
driver, too, was ready to undergo his fate right at this moment? In
other words, karmic retribution is no simple process, but a network
of numerous strands, which yet somehow succeed in attaining a just
result. How is that done?

In view of all these difficulties, one might well wonder whether
the belief in rebirth and karmic retribution can be reasonably enter-
tained. No Indian philosophers—with the exception of the Carvakas,
mentioned earlier—were willing to give it up, however. They felt that
the variety that characterizes living beings is a confirmation of this
belief, for how could it be explained otherwise? Shankara, the Advaita thinker whom we met above, states this explicitly in his commentary on the *Brahma Sutra* (2.1.35). Considering how this variety
might have come about if we assume that God created the world out
of an earlier state in which there were no distinctions, he points out
that God did not create the world out of such an earlier state: the cycle of rebirths is without beginning so that there was always earlier
karma to explain the variety in each next creation.

There is another factor that endeared the belief in rebirth and
karmic retribution to many, including philosophers. This belief gave
moral structure to the world. It implied that good deeds, often in
spite of appearances, will lead to good results and that bad deeds will
be punished. The *Mahabharata* puts it this way (13.6.19): "If one's actions bore no fruit, then everything would be of no avail," and this
was no doubt a sentiment shared by many.

The belief in rebirth and karmic retribution, then, provided a
sense of intelligibility to India's philosophers and a sense of justice
not only to them but to many others as well. All of them accepted this
notion, and no one was ready to abandon it.

We know that from the early centuries of the Common Era onward, a number of philosophical schools existed side by side in India
that tried to present an intelligible picture of the world we live in and
of our place in it. These thinkers were bound to be confronted with
the question of how karma "works," and they made efforts to tackle

this problem. However, the problem was daunting, and the attempts to solve it took different forms. What is more, before they could even consider any solution, these philosophers had to be clear about what kind of solution might be deemed acceptable.

This last issue needs some explanation. The Indian thinkers who occupied themselves with the workings of karma were faced with the question of teleology. That is to say, they had to decide whether and to what extent an explanation in terms of purposes is acceptable. Human and animal behavior is frequently explained in terms of its purpose—for example, "the cat lies in wait *in order to* catch a mouse"—and few people would object to this. However, this kind of explanation becomes problematic when applied to lifeless objects. Can one really say that the sun shines *in order to* bring light to the world? Those who maintain this in all seriousness may use this expression to state that a conscious being created the sun for this purpose; the purpose belongs in this case to the creator, not to the unconscious object, the sun, which he or she created. In other words, the attribution of purpose to lifeless objects or mechanisms is far from obvious and may be objected to in principle.

Modern scientific thought does indeed object in principle to explanations in terms of *final causes,* or purposes. The fame of Charles Darwin is not based on the fact that he discovered evolution (he did not), but on the fact that he found a way to explain it without needing final causes: he took the purposefulness out of biological evolution. Certain psychologists, too, see it as their task to explain even human behavior in terms that are, in the end, nonteleological.

What did the Indian philosophers think about final causes? The answer is that different thinkers held different opinions on this matter. The Sankhya school of philosophy, to begin with, had no scruples using final causes, at least in its classical text, the *Sankhya Karika.* Remember that Sankhya distinguished between the self (one self for each animate being) and Original Nature. The latter of these two gives rise to composite objects, and this, verse 17 maintains, constitutes proof for the existence of the self: "The self exists because composite objects are *for something else*...and because there is activity *for the sake of* its isolation." Isolation, it may be recalled, is the isolation of the self, its liberation. Original Nature and its derivatives act so as to bring about this isolation. In other words, they pursue an aim, they are teleological in spite of the fact that they are unconscious.

Verse 21, too, introduces a teleological element in the following charming comparison: "The contact between self and nature, which is like the contact between a lame man and a blind man, is *for the sake of* seeing in the case of the self and *for the sake of* isolation in the case of nature." The comparison evokes the picture of a blind man who carries a lame man; they both profit from this arrangement. But the goal-directedness of this arrangement is also ascribed to the self and to nature, which some (but not the Sankhyas) might consider a dubious procedure.

Is there a possibility to account for karmic retribution without recourse to teleology? Most thinkers of classical India were confronted with this question, for only few—most notably the Sankhyas—were willing to accept final causes in this matter.

A simple if somewhat strange solution to the problem of karmic retribution was provided by thinkers of the Sarvastivada school of thought. Recall that this school owed its name to the doctrine that past and future things exist. A consequence of this position is that past deeds exist at the moment when they carry fruit. No teleological action is therefore required. Actions do not have to steer future events so as to lead to an appropriate retribution of deeds carried out long ago, for those actions are there at the moment of retribution.

A similar solution was presented by other representatives of Sankhya thought, all of whom were apparently not satisfied with the readiness of some of their colleagues to use a teleological explanation. These other Sankhya thinkers invoked a doctrine that the school had accepted to respond to a different set of problems, the *satkarya-vada,* the doctrine according to which the effect exists in the cause (see the boxed text titled "Shared Problems in Indian Philosophy"). Applied to deeds and their results, this doctrine implies that the results are in a certain sense present in the deeds that cause them. This solution, if it is one, does circumvent the problem of teleology, to be sure, but it leaves numerous other questions unanswered.

Shared Problems in Indian Philosophy

Presentations of the history of Indian philosophy often depict the different schools of thought as if they were and remained independent of each other, each developing its views with little or no interference from the other schools. Historically this is not correct. Philosophers from different schools were aware of the ideas current in other schools than their own, if for no other reason than that they might sometimes be challenged to defend their views against those of another school. What is more, such debates could be public, held in the presence of the king or his representative, and the loser of the debate could lose the respect and support of the political ruler or even his life.

Most philosophical schools, moreover, shared a number of ideals and convictions. The most important ideal was liberation, and all schools (with the exceptions of Mimamsa until the sixth century and Carvaka until its disappearance toward the end of the first millennium C.E.) subscribed to this ideal. The accompanying conviction was the belief in rebirth and karmic retribution, and karmic retribution presented a challenge to Indian philosophers that none of them, irrespective of the specific school or religion they belonged to, could ignore. In a presentation of the history of Indian philosophy, it is therefore vital to be aware of the problems these thinkers shared, even if in all other respects they strongly disagreed with each other and would deal with these shared problems in entirely different ways.

Among the other problems that all Indian philosophies shared, one turned out to be of particular importance: the correspondence between words and things. All Brahmanical schools took such a correspondence for granted. This is not surprising in view of the fact that they held on to an ancient language, Sanskrit, which they considered the only real and beginningless language, all other languages being no more than corruptions of this eternal language. In their view, there was a timeless harmony between Sanskrit and reality, and the correspondence between words and things was for them a matter of course. The Buddhists, unlike the Brahmins, thought of Sanskrit as just one language among others. Moreover, they developed the idea that the world of our experience hides a deeper reality. They did not therefore assign ultimate reality to the objects of our daily experience: houses, pots, chariots, but also persons. In fact, they appealed to language (any language) to explain that we, in our practical lives, have the mistaken view that the world is populated with houses, pots, chariots, and persons: we believe in their existence because we have words for them.

In spite of their differences, both Brahmins and Buddhists (as well as Jainas who joined the debate) had difficulties making sense of certain propositions. Ordinary propositions—like "the man reads a book"—could be thought of as designating a situation that is constituted of the items referred to by their words. And indeed, the proposition "the man reads a book" designates a situation in which there are a man, a book, and the activity of reading (in Sanskrit and Middle Indic languages there are no articles corresponding to English *the* and *a*.) Other propositions, however, could not be understood in this manner because they designate situations in which not all the items referred to by their words are present. The situation designated by "the potter makes a pot" contains a potter and the activity of making but no pot. Indeed, if it contained a pot, there would be no need to make one.

Different thinkers came up with different solutions to the problems evoked by propositions of this kind. Many Buddhists were happy to conclude that these conceived contradictions merely showed that the world of our experience is self-contradictory and cannot be real in any absolute sense. This was a position they had held so far without proof (see the boxed text titled "Buddhist Scholasticism and the Beginning of Indian Philosophy") but for which they now believed to have solid proof. For many Brahmanical thinkers the situation was much more irksome because they were not ready to abandon the reality of the world of our experience. Some of them, most particularly the Sankhyas, thought it unavoidable

to conclude that there somehow was a pot in the situation designated by "the potter makes a pot": this pot must then be present in the clay that obviously is there when the potter makes
a pot. In other words, they held the doctrine that the effect is
present in the cause, in Sanskrit, *satkarya-vada*. Others came
up with different, equally daring solutions, which cannot all be
discussed here. It is, however, undeniable that this shared problem exerted a determining influence on the shapes that the different schools of Indian philosophy came to adopt.

Other solutions to the problem of karmic retribution were, however, possible. Consider the Buddhist position (excepting the Sarvastivada). Buddhist scholastic thinkers had come to the position that
the karmically productive aspect of the deeds we carry out is their
mental aspect. That is to say, it is not so much the physical aspect of
our deeds that is responsible for karmic retribution, but rather the
state of mind in which they are carried out. We know that desire
plays a crucial role already in early Buddhism, so much so that the
way to liberation passes through the destruction of desire. Another
aspect of acts that the Buddhists consider karmically operative is intention. The mental nature of intention, like that of desire, needs no
explanation.

Deeds leave traces in the mind, more precisely in the series of
mind-events that the Buddhists believe constitute the mental con-
tinuum. It follows that deeds, which are mental, leave traces that are
mental. The next question to be asked is: is the fruition of deeds also
mental?

The Buddhist scholastic position was that they are not, or not exclusively. Deeds are mental, the traces they leave are mental, but their
fruition is not only mental. Indeed, these thinkers were convinced
that the universe in all its vastness is the result of the deeds of living beings.

The difficulties connected with this position are hardly in need
of elucidation. How should we imagine that the series of mind-
events that constitute animate beings determine what happens outside them in the material world? Buddhist philosophers were aware

of this problem, and this is most clearly illustrated by considering the case of one of their most prominent thinkers, Vasubandhu. Vasubandhu composed the *Abhidharmakosha Bhashya,* a text that we have come across several times already. This same Vasubandhu, according to a legend that might contain historical truth, changed his mind on certain points later in life. This change of mind finds expression in a short treatise of twenty verses, the *Vimshatika,* which he presumably composed at that time, along with a commentary from his own hand. In this commentary, verse 7, Vasubandhu raises the following question: "The impression of a deed enters into the series of consciousness, nowhere else. Why don't you accept that the fruition comes about right there where the impression is and is therefore a corresponding modification of consciousness? What is the reason that you imagine the fruition of an impression to come about there, where the impression is not?" This question hits the nail on the head, so to say. It formulates the problem in the clearest possible terms. How and why are we to imagine that series of mental events shape the outside world? Why don't we simply grant that karmic retribution, like the deeds and the traces that give rise to it, is a mental affair?

However, there is a hitch. What happens to the effect of karma on the universe, including the material universe? The position that Vasubandhu and certain other Buddhist thinkers take is as follows. Yes, the deeds of living beings are responsible for the universe in all its details, but like deeds, the so-called material universe is mental, too. These Buddhists adopted in this manner a position that deserves to be called idealism. As some Buddhist texts put it: "Whatever belongs to the Triple World is nothing but mind."

By claiming that the entire universe is essentially mental in nature, these Buddhists succeeded in reducing the whole karmic process to what we might call a psychological process: a psychological act leaves psychological traces, which in their turn bring about a psychological effect. Bringing about a psychological effect is not dissimilar to producing a dream; and while the details of this process may remain complex, it will be clear that karmic retribution is in this case infinitely less difficult to explain than in the case where a psychological trace is believed to determine the shape and development of the physical universe. These Buddhists were not the only ones to opt for this solution. Certain later Brahmanical authors did the same and did not hesitate to compare the world to a dream.

It goes without saying that the psychological explanation of karmic retribution could not but have much appeal for those who saw it as their task to explain its mechanism. This appeal was not limited to those who were ready to deny the universe an independent, material reality, even though the task was easiest for them. Others, too, tried this solution.

A striking example is Shabara, the author of the oldest surviving commentary in the field of Vedic hermeneutics (Mimamsa) who lived around the middle of the first millennium C.E. and who, surprisingly, showed no interest in the doctrine of rebirth and karmic retribution. However, he *was* concerned with the effects of certain acts, that is, sacrificial acts. Vedic injunctions often state that a correctly executed sacrifice leads to heaven. Rebirth and "ordinary" karmic retribution do not come into the picture, but obviously there had to be some causal chain that led from the performed sacrifice to its effect, heaven. This causal chain preoccupied Shabara's mind, and he had a great deal to say about it.

Interestingly, Shabara psychologizes the process from beginning to end. That is to say, he claims that the really effective part of the sacrifice is the psychological attitude that accompanies it. He further claims that the traces that are left by the sacrifice are psychological by nature. And on top of all this, he states that heaven is not some place where one might go after death, but happiness. Shabara does not stop here. What he says about the deities who are supposed to be the recipients of the sacrifice shows that he looks upon them as mere names. In other words, every single element in the process that leads from the sacrifice to its reward is psychological.

Shabara's case is striking but strictly speaking only marginally connected with the question of rebirth and karmic retribution: Shabara does not appear to believe in rebirth and is not concerned with the effect of deeds other than the sacrificial act. Moreover, he did not claim or believe that sacrificial effects are responsible for the universe we live in. Unlike some of the thinkers we have considered above, he did not therefore feel compelled to reduce the universe to psychology. Differently put, he was under no pressure to opt for idealism as a philosophical position.

There were, however, other thinkers, who did believe in rebirth and karmic retribution but did not feel inclined to idealism, and who yet felt attracted to a psychological explanation of the process. Was there any chance for them to succeed?

In order to consider one attempt of this nature, let us recall that, in the Vaisheshika scheme of things, merit *(dharma)* and demerit *(adharma)* are responsible for karmic retribution. The question these thinkers had to address is, how can they do so? Let us not forget that merit and demerit have no intelligence of their own. They are qualities of the self, to be sure, but the self derives its intelligence from another quality, consciousness. This consciousness does not guide merit and demerit in their search for karmic retribution. Indeed, in cases where karmic retribution is unpleasant for the person concerned, one would expect that its intelligence will do what it can to avoid that outcome. What, then, allows merit and demerit to bring about appropriate results, very often in a future life?

At this point the option of a psychological explanation presents itself. The question would indeed be relatively easy to answer if *dharma* did nothing beyond bringing about a pleasant experience and if *adharma* merely brought about an unpleasant experience. After all, *dharma* and *adharma* are qualities of the self, as are positive and negative experiences. If the qualities *dharma* and *adharma* merely produced the qualities pleasure and pain in the same self, this would be a process internal to one single self. The temptation to think of karmic retribution in these terms was great, as will be clear from the following passage from a text (the *Nyaya Sutra* and *Bhashya*) that is close to Vaisheshika:

[Objection:] Because the substrates are different, the comparison with the appearance of a fruit in a tree does not explain the link between deeds and their effects.

Tending the tree—that is, watering its roots and so forth—and the fruit both have the tree as substrate; deeds, in contrast, take place in this world, in the body, while their results belong to the next world. It follows that the comparison with the appearance of a fruit in a tree does not explain the link between deeds and their effects because the substrates are different.

[Reply:] This objection is not valid because pleasure has the self as substrate.

Pleasure, being experienced by the self, has the self as substrate. *Dharma* has the very same self as substrate because *dharma* is a quality of the self. It follows that it is not correct to state that deeds and their effects have different substrates.

[Objection:] This is not correct because material objects such as sons, cattle, women, property, gold, and food have been indicated in the Veda to be the results of karma.

Sons and the like, not pleasure, have been indicated as being the results of karma in Vedic injunctions such as "he who desires a village should sacrifice" and "he who desires a son should sacrifice." It follows that what has been stated above to the extent that pleasure is the result of karma is incorrect.

[Reply:] Because the result comes about by virtue of a connection with those things, they are metaphorically called result.

The result, that is, pleasure, comes about by virtue of a connection with sons and so forth. For this reason sons and so forth are metaphorically called the results of karma, just as the word *breath* is metaphorically applied to food in the statement "breath is indeed food."

Unfortunately, this explanation is not very satisfactory. Consider the hypothetical car accident evoked earlier. Here more is involved than the mere individual karmic retributions of the two drivers. Their karmic strands are intertwined, but this is only the beginning of the problem. If the accident was, say, the result of a slippery road surface, which karmic strand made the road slippery? And if it was the result of distraction caused by a passenger, whose karma induced that passenger to act in a manner so as to distract the driver? Many more questions like these could be asked. They make us understand that the image of the fruit in the tree one has tended does no justice to karmic retribution as it is supposed to take place in the real world (assuming, for arguments' sake, that karma is responsible for all, or almost all, that happens).

The Vaisheshika thinkers were aware of all this. They also realized that they could not solve the issue mechanically. That is to say, they discovered that no easy mechanical explanation could be found for karmic retribution. What they ended up doing amounted more or less to a betrayal of their initial philosophical aspirations and an abandonment of the psychological explanation: they postulated the existence of a creator God who would arrange things in accordance with the past deeds of living beings.

Prashastapada, who lived in the sixth century C.E., may have been the first to introduce the notion of a creator God into Vaisheshika. He does so in the following passage, while describing the process of creation:

> When the four composite elements have come into existence, a Great Egg is formed, caused solely by God's volition, out of atoms of fire with an admixture of atoms of earth [i.e., out of gold]. In it God creates Brahma, with four faces like so many lotuses, the grandfather of all worlds, and all worlds; he then enjoins him with the duty of creating living things. That Brahma, thus enjoined by God and endowed with abundant knowledge, complete absence of passion, and absolute power, *knows the effects of the deeds of living beings;* he creates various gods and the other living beings; he then connects them with *dharma,* knowledge, absence of passion, and power *in accordance with their residue of past deeds.*

It is clear from this passage that God's role, as envisaged by Prashastapada, is essentially that of an accountant: he keeps count of all the good and bad deeds of all sentient beings and rewards or punishes them accordingly. Vaisheshika had a need for such a God, for otherwise it could not explain the workings of karmic retribution. Indeed, another thinker, Jayanta Bhatta, who lived a few centuries later, turns this need to understand into a proof for the existence of God:

> The variety of the world is not possible without the workings of the deeds of living beings; that is why it is generally assumed that deeds, even though one does not see them while they effect their results, are its cause. Such being the case, since it is not possible to produce such effects on the basis of unconscious agents that

are not even guided by an animate being, a conscious agent that guides them must equally be assumed.

From a philosophical point of view, the introduction of an accountant God was not very satisfactory. The Vaisheshikas ended up understanding, however, that without such a God they could get nowhere close to an understanding of karmic retribution. Skeptics will no doubt observe that the introduction of God did not solve the problem either: instead of solving the problem, they gave a name to it, "God." The attraction of this solution, real or imagined, must yet have been considerable at a time when the worship of a highest God had come to occupy an important place in the religious life of many Indians. And it is not surprising that some of those religiously inclined people had already made the link between God and karmic retribution well before the philosophers of the Vaisheshika school felt compelled to do so.

An example of a religious text that describes God as "the supervisor of karma" is the *Shvetashvatara Upanishad.* This text may have been composed in the early centuries of the Common Era (see the boxed text titled "The Veda") and contains the following verse (6.1): "The one God, hidden in all beings, all-pervading and yet the interior self of all beings, *is the supervisor of karma,* the dwelling place of all beings, the witness, the judge, isolated, and free from material parts." The *Laws of Manu,* a text dating from around the same period, personalizes the process of karmic retribution by introducing two somewhat obscure "beings of great power" (12.18–19): "Unwearied, these two jointly examine the dead man's merits and sins, linked to which one secures happiness or suffering here and in the hereafter." The feature that strikes us in the Vaisheshika conception of God, as noted above, is that this God is no more than an accountant. His own opinion about the deeds of living beings is totally irrelevant in His activity of apportioning reward and punishment. The famous philosopher Shankara, though a Vedantin and not a Vaisheshika, deals with this same issue in his commentary on *Brahma Sutra* 2.1.34. He there states: "The creation is uneven in accordance with the merit and demerit of the creatures; for this, God cannot be blamed." Indeed, it would be hard to blame God for anything, given that He does little beyond applying rules that He has not Himself ordained or invented. God's omniscience, according to Shankara on *Bhagavadgita* 7.22, is explained by the fact that He knows the classification of karma and its fruition. And the same commentary on *Bhagavadgita* 8.9 characterizes God as "upholder of all," this because He is "the creator/organizer of the whole collection of karmic fruits, the distributor of them to the living beings in all their variety." These and other passages show that many thinkers were content to think of God as, in the end, limited in His power by external rules, such as the rules of karmic retribution. We will see in a future chapter that not everyone was happy with this.

The Vaisheshikas, as we know, accepted God as the explanation for the renewed creation of the world in accordance with the deeds of living beings carried out in the preceding world period. They avoided in this manner the problem that had almost unhinged the Sankhya philosophy. Did they invoke God also to explain karmic retribution within one single world period? Is God the one who steers things so as to end up with the car accident discussed above? Many philosophers of the Vaisheshika and related schools no doubt came to agree on this. However, they do not always emphasize it, and it seems licit to suppose that at least some of them remained ill at ease with an explanation that they may have thought of as an admission of defeat.

PART II

VARIANTS OF KARMA

CHAPTER 5

Transfer of Merit

Rebirth and karmic retribution are a private affair. Living beings reap the consequences of what they have themselves done, not of what others have done. Only in this way does it make sense to look for escape from rebirth and karmic retribution in a highly individualized fashion, for example, by practicing asceticism or by finding out the true nature of one's self.

Various texts give expression to the fundamentally individual nature of karmic retribution. The following passage is from a Brahmanical text, the *Brahma Purana* (217.1–16):

> The sages asked Vyasa: "Who is the companion of a dying man, his father or mother or son or teacher, his crowd of friends and relations? When he leaves the body that has been his house as if it were a house of wood or mud, and goes into the world beyond, who follows him?" The sage Vyasa replied: "Alone he is born, and alone he dies; alone he crosses the dangerous thresholds, without the companionship of father, mother, brother, son, or teacher, without his crowd of friends and relations. When he leaves the dead body, for a brief moment he weeps, and then he turns his face away and departs. When he leaves the body, virtue alone follows him; if he has virtue he goes to heaven, but if he has sin he goes to hell. Earth, wind, space, water, light, mind, intelligence, and the self—these are the witnesses that watch constantly over the virtue of creatures that breathe on earth; together with them, virtue follows the soul. Skin, bone, flesh, semen, and blood leave the body

when it is lifeless; but the soul that has virtue prospers happily in the world and the world beyond."

We must assume that the change from a collective vision of society to a vision that centered on the individual was bound to create difficulties, especially in the Brahmanical tradition. The message of the *Bhagavadgita* attempted to bring the two into agreement, by pointing out that well-adjusted social behavior (following Brahmanical norms) was the best way to attain liberation from rebirth and karmic retribution. Others dealt with the problem differently, by giving a different twist to the idea of karmic retribution. They maintained that the store of karmic residue that someone has accumulated may affect someone else. We speak in that case of transfer of merit (or demerit).

It may not be possible to determine with certainty where and when the notion of gaining merit through transfer and of incurring demerit in a parallel fashion originated. The notion of transferring merit to deceased ancestors may have absorbed elements from the Vedic custom (called *shraddha*) of ritually feeding the ancestors. Inscriptional and other evidence indicates that the belief in transfer of merit became extremely popular in all denominations, including Buddhism and Jainism. Yet it is clear that the notion exerted a particular attraction on Brahmanism. (Buddhism and Jainism never came to terms with this belief on a theoretical level.) It is in the texts of the Brahmanical tradition that we find it invoked on several occasions. An early example is the *Brihadaranyaka Upanishad* (6.4.3):

> Her vulva is the sacrificial ground; her pubic hair is the sacred grass; her labia majora are the Soma-press; and her labia minora are the fire blazing at the center. A man who engages in sexual intercourse with this knowledge obtains as great a world as a man who performs a Soma sacrifice, and *he appropriates to himself the good deeds* of the women with whom he has sex. The women, for their part, *appropriate to themselves the good deeds* of a man who engages in sexual intercourse with them without this knowledge.

Another Upanishad—the *Kaushitaki Upanishad* (2.15)—illustrates a more generalized transfer, not only of deeds:

Next, the father-son ceremony, which is also called the rite of transfer. A father, when he is close to death, calls his son. After the house has been strewn with fresh grass, the fire has been kindled, and a pot of water has been set down along with a cup, the father lies down covered in a fresh garment. The son comes and lies on top of him, touching the various organs of the father with his own corresponding organs. Alternatively, the father may execute the transfer with the son sitting and facing him. The father then makes the transfer to the son:

"I will place my speech in you," says the father. "I place your speech in me," responds the son.

"I will place my breath in you," says the father. "I place your breath in me," responds the son.

"I will place my sight in you," says the father. "I place your sight in me," responds the son.

"I will place my hearing in you," says the father. "I place your hearing in me," responds the son.

"I will place my tasting of food in you," says the father. "I place your tasting of food in me," responds the son.

"I will place my actions in you," says the father. "I place your actions in me," responds the son.

"I will place my pleasures and pains in you," says the father. "I place your pleasures and pains in me," responds the son.... If he finds it difficult to talk, the father should say very briefly: "I will place my vital functions in you." And the son should respond: "I place your vital functions in me."...

If the father recovers his health, he should either live under the authority of his son or live as a wandering ascetic. But if he happens to die, they should perform the appropriate rites for him.

A passage from the *Mahabharata* (1.75.2) states in so many words that the effects of sin may affect other members of one's family: "The perpetration of lawlessness does not like a cow yield results instantly. But evil does bear sure fruit, like a heavy meal on the stomach; if you do not see it ripen on yourself, it will on your sons or grandsons." The *Laws of Manu,* a text which we have already come across, provides further illustrations of karmic transfer. We read here, for example (6.79): "Consigning his good deeds to people he likes and his evil deeds to people he dislikes, he attains the eternal Brahma through the practice of meditation." And again (7.94–95): "When a man is killed in battle by the enemy as he turns tail frightened, he takes upon himself all the evil deeds committed by his master; while any good deeds that a man killed as he turns tail has stored up for the hereafter, all of that his master takes from him"; "When a Brahmin resides somewhere without being treated with respect, he takes away all the good works of even a man who makes daily offerings in the five sacred fires" (3.100); "He must never bathe in a reservoir that belongs to someone else. By doing so, he will be tainted with a portion of the evils committed by the man who constructed the reservoir" (4.201). And finally (8.316–317): "Whether he is punished or released, the thief is released from the theft; but if the king fails to punish him, he takes upon himself the thief's guilt. The murderer of a learned Brahmin rubs his sin off on the man who eats his food, an adulterous wife on her husband, a pupil and a patron of a sacrifice on the teacher, and a thief on the king."

The practical consequences of the transfer of merit and demerit in these last cases can be compared to the message of the *Bhagavadgita*. There as here the soldier must fight; the king must distribute justice. If they don't, they are not on the road to liberation in the *Bhagavadgita*, they risk disagreeable future lives in the *Laws of Manu*. The mechanism in the two texts is altogether different: The *Bhagavadgita* adheres to the notion of deeds clinging to the person who has committed them; the *Laws of Manu* uses the alternative notion that the result of good deeds, merit, can be lost, and the outcome of bad deeds of others, demerit, may become attached to oneself.

Certain ascetics from among the followers of the god Shiva made a peculiar use of the transfer of merit and demerit. Their aim was to create social situations in which their own demerit would be taken over by others, and the merit of those others would accrue to them. Such situations could be created by the irregular behavior that these ascetics cultivated. They would behave in socially unacceptable and disgusting ways, thus evoking the ire of bystanders. They might in this way be verbally and physically abused, but this was in a way the aim of the exercise. The dishonor they were subjected to by those others meant that the others' merit came to them, while their own demerit moved into the abusers.

The belief in transfer of merit and demerit was not confined to Brahmanism. It appears to have become (or may always have been) part of popular religion and to have found in this manner its way into all the major religions of classical India. Numerous Buddhist donations, for example, have as goal to transfer the merit acquired to this or that (often deceased) member of the family, even though theoretically Buddhism was ill at ease with this notion.

Transfer of merit has an important place in a development of Buddhism commonly known by the name Mahayana. Certain Buddhists were keen not just to strive for liberation, but decided to become buddhas themselves. This is a far higher aim, which demands much more from aspirants than mere liberation does. Those ready to make the effort, which might require millions and billions of future lives, would take a vow to pursue the path to buddhahood to the end. They were henceforth bodhisattvas, future buddhas. During their long and difficult journey toward full enlightenment, bodhisattvas take on the suffering of others and transfer their own merits to them.

Theoretically transfer of merit does not appear to have found entry into Jainism. This did not, however, stop many Jainas from letting in this notion through a back door, so to say, for example, by performing rituals meant to reduce hindrances for deceased relatives.

Theoretically the transfer of merit remained problematic even for Brahmins who had accepted karmic retribution. Consider, for example, the following passage from the *Mahabharata* (13.6.9–10): "He who acts will himself experience the result of his activity, whether good or bad; this is directly perceived in the world. Pure action brings forth happiness. Suffering comes from evil action. In all cases one obtains what one has done; one will never experience what one has not done." This passage emphasizes the individual nature of karmic retribution. The same chapter of the *Mahabharata*, however, also contains the following verse: "In former times the mythical character Yayati had failed in heaven, been thrown out by the gods, and fallen down on earth. By meritorious acts of his daughter's sons, however, he was raised again to heaven." These contrasting passages in one single chapter suggest that theoretical and practical beliefs were not always in agreement.

The same was true for Buddhism. In this case, however, the transfer of merit, though determining the religious practice of most lay people and monastics had little theoretical attraction. The following statement, from the Buddhist philosopher called Bhavya (sixth century C.E.?), may therefore be considered representative of educated Buddhist thought: "It is inconceivable that sin be transferred from the soul of one person to that of another. This is because sin is not something material. Likewise, desire, hatred and delusion, and so forth, cannot be transferred from one soul to another. One can be sure that it is not possible to give and receive good and bad karma. This is because karma is bound up with the mind. The same goes for pleasure and pain." We know that, in spite of these kinds of considerations, transfer of merit was at the center of Buddhism as it was practiced by most of its followers, whether lay or monastic.

CHAPTER 6

Competitors of Karma

The importance of karma is emphasized in texts belonging to both Brahmanism and Buddhism. A chapter of the *Padma Purana* (2.94), to take an example from the Brahmanical tradition, claims that karma is the cause of everything that happens in the universe. And the Buddhist *Abhidharmakosha Bhashya* of Vasubandhu states in so many words that "the diversity in the world is born from karma"; other passages add that this includes the very structure of the universe. This does not entitle us to conclude that everyone in the Brahmanical and Buddhist traditions attributed quite so much importance to karma (not everyone did), but it does illustrate the central place that karma occupied in Indian thought.

In spite of this, earlier deeds are not always presented as the only factor that determines present events. Present experiences are frequently stated to be the result of other factors, often banal ones such as the state of one's health, the weather, excessive indulgence in unwholesome substances, or violence. A passage from the Buddhist canon (*Samyutta Nikaya* IV, pp. 230–231), which records a discussion between the Buddha and a wanderer called Sivaka, illustrates this:

> "Master Gotama, there are some ascetics and Brahmins who hold such a doctrine and view as this: 'Whatever a person experiences, whether it be pleasant or painful or neither-painful-nor-pleasant, all that is caused by what was done in the past.' What does Master Gotama say about this?"
>
> "Some feelings, Sivaka, arise here originating from bile disor-

ders: that some feelings arise from bile disorders one can know for oneself, and that is considered to be true in the world. Now when those ascetics and Brahmins hold such a doctrine and view as this, 'Whatever a person experiences, whether it be pleasant or painful or neither-painful-nor-pleasant, all that is caused by what was done in the past,' they overshoot what one knows by oneself and they overshoot what is considered to be true in the world. Therefore I say that this is wrong on the part of those ascetics and Brahmins.

Some feelings, Sivaka, arise here originating from phlegm disorders... originating from wind disorders... originating from an imbalance of the three... produced by change of climate... produced by careless behavior... caused by assault... produced as the result of karma: that some feelings arise here produced as the result of karma one can know for oneself, and that is considered to be true in the world. Now when those ascetics and Brahmins hold such a doctrine and view as this, 'Whatever a person experiences, whether it be pleasant or painful or neither-painful-nor-pleasant, all that is caused by what was done in the past,' they overshoot what one knows by oneself and they overshoot what is considered to be true in the world. Therefore I say that this is wrong on the part of those ascetics and Brahmins."

Further factors are enumerated in Brahmanical texts. An example is the *Shvetashvatara Upanishad* (6.1), which states: "Some wise men say it is one's own nature, while others say it is time—all totally deluded. It is rather the greatness of God present in the world by means of which this wheel of Brahma goes about." The *Bhagavata Purana* (4.11.21–25) gives a longer list: "The Lord ordains the increase or decrease in the life span of a miserable creature. Some say this is karma; others that it is one's own nature; others that it is time; others that it is fate; and others that it is desire." From among these factors, the *nature* here referred to may well be the nature also invoked by the Carvakas in order to explain the diversity of the world we live in. Of more interest at present are time and fate. Before turning to them, we will consider the role of curses.

Curses were a special concern of the Brahmins. Recall that the extraordinary powers that they claimed to possess most often found expression in their use of magical formulas, among them precisely curses. A curse might have a profound effect on its victim. There are countless stories in Brahmanical literature that illustrate this. The best known of these stories is about Shakuntala, a girl who fell in love with the king and secretly married him. Absorbed in thought after this event, she did not pay proper attention to a passing Brahmanical sage, who felt offended and pronounced the curse that the object of her thought would forget her. And indeed, when Shakuntala went some time later to the court to present her newborn infant to his father, the king had forgotten all about their encounter. This led to great complications, which it took a long time to resolve. This mythological motive inspired the great Sanskrit poet Kalidasa to compose his most famous drama, much admired by readers around the world (including the famous German author Johann Wolfgang von Goethe [1749–1832]). The question that concerns us here is not how the problem was resolved, but how it could come about in the first place. Was this curse the consequence of a sin committed by Shakuntala in an earlier life? Was it the result of karmic retribution?

Our sources are silent on this particular case. However, there are many instances where they show a certain unease with regard to curses. This is not surprising, for curses and karmic retribution often seem incompatible. If a person's fate can be affected by the fact that a curse has been pronounced against him or her, does this mean that the law of karmic retribution can be manipulated at will by the sages and Brahmins who pronounced it? Moreover, while some curses are justified, others are not. The most trifling offense often provokes the most terrible curse. So how can curses and karmic retribution be brought into agreement?

There is a clear tendency in the development of Indian literature to try to bridge the gap between these two. Curses tend to fit in more and more with what one might expect on the basis of moral (i.e., karmic) considerations. At first sight inexplicable disasters that befall hapless victims come to be explained by invoking well-deserved curses, sometimes in earlier lives. Curses and karmic retribution thus come to work in tandem, the former giving concrete shape to the just deserts of the person cursed.

While the efficacy of curses was something that the Brahmins were not keen to give up, the idea of fatalism, that is, a strict determinism that leaves no room for freedom of decision, is known in the first place from Ajivikism. According to this religion, each individual has to pass through a stupendously long series of births, and there is nothing he or she can do about this. It must be added that, at least in the case of Ajivikism, this determinism was at bottom a karmic determinism: earlier deeds compel us to act as we do, and these new deeds determine our future. We also saw that a similar element of determinism was part of the message of the *Bhagavadgita*. Here, to be sure, this determinism steers the body when a person has realized his or her own different identity.

Fatalism also appears independently, primarily in the *Mahabharata*, and is there frequently associated with Time. Time is presented as destiny, or fate, and human beings are quite helpless against it. The attitude that the epic preaches in the face of destiny is acceptance (3.245.13–15):

A person experiences pleasure and pain in turn; no one obtains total lack of pleasure. A wise person, who has the highest insight and is aware of life's ups and downs does not grieve, nor does he rejoice. He should experience pleasure when it comes and tolerate pain when it comes. He should respect what Time [i.e., destiny] brings, like a farmer who respects his crops.

And again (1.84.6):

In the world of the living many creatures depend on fate, and their acts are wasted—whatever he gets, the sage should not bother; soul's wisdom knows that his fate is stronger.

Sometimes the epic contrasts fate and human effort, the latter of these two being karma. An example is the following passage (*Mahabharata* 13.6.5–11):

Nothing is born without seed; without seed there can be no fruit. From seed arises seed. It is known that fruit comes only from seed.
    Just as a farmer plants a certain kind of seed and gets a certain crop, so it is with good and bad deeds.

Just as a field sown without seed is barren, so without human effort there is no fate.

The field is seen to be the effort of a person, while fate is the seed. From the union of field and seed a crop flourishes.

The doer himself enjoys the fruit of his action. This is seen clearly in the world in regard to activity and inactivity.

Happiness comes through pure actions; suffering results from evil actions. By action, all things are obtained. By inaction, nothing whatever is enjoyed.

In all cases, a doer who is harmed by fate does not get knocked off base, while a non-doer gets a sprinkling of salt in his wound.

In spite of the contrast here expressed, the opposition between fatalism and karmic retribution is not quite as stark as that between curses and karmic retribution. The two coexisted most harmoniously in Ajivikism and in a way also in the *Bhagavadgita*. It is even possible that fatalism came about as a particular interpretation of karmic retribution. And indeed, the doctrine of karmic retribution, if interpreted strictly, can lead to fatalism. To borrow the words of the *Matsya Purana* (221.1–12): "One's own karma is called fate, earned from another body."

Also a medical treatise, the *Caraka Samhita* (3.3.30), states that fate and karma amount to the same: "Fate is to be regarded as self-inflicted, an action [karma] of a prior incarnation." However, it introduces a new element that can be used to offset the effects of karma: medicine. More generally, there is such a thing as human effort that can counter the effects that previous karma would bring about. For example, karma might favor a certain life span, but this karmic life span is not fixed. The *Caraka Samhita* (3.3.36) elaborates this as follows:

If all life spans were fixed, then in search of good health none would employ efficacious remedies or magical formulas, herbs, precious stones, amulets, offerings, oblations, observances, expiations, fasting, benedictions, and prostrations. There would be no disturbed, ferocious, or ill-mannered cattle, elephants, camels, donkeys, horses, buffalos, and the like, and nothing such as polluted winds to be avoided. No anxiety about falling from moun-

tains or rough impassible waters; and none whose minds were
negligent, insane, disturbed, fierce, ill-mannered, foolish, avari-
cious, and lowborn; no enemies, no raging fires, and none of the
various poisonous creepers and snakes; no violent acts, no actions
out of place or untimely, no kingly wrath. For the occurrence of
these and the like would not cause death if the term of all life were
fixed and predetermined.

The same text (ibid.) then takes recourse to observation to prove that
life spans cannot be fixed:

It is by observing that we perceive the following: over the course
of a great many battles, the life span of the thousands of men who
fight compared with those who don't is not the same; similarly
for those who treat every medical condition that may arise ver-
sus those who don't. There is also a discrepancy in the life span of
those who imbibe poison and those who do not. Jugs for drinking
water and ornamental jugs do not last the same amount of time;
consequently, duration of life is based on salutary practices, and
from the antithesis there is death.

While discussing the presentation of karma in the Puranas, we came
across the notion of expiation, which figured prominently in those
texts. Expiation is a notion that in its earliest manifestations is inseparable from the Vedic ritual. Rituals have to be carried out without fault, for faults risk reducing the value of a ritual to naught. They
still happen, so measures were taken to repair such faults. These were
the expiations, self-imposed activities of a specific kind that were believed to undo the faults.

Expiations remained popular within the Brahmanical tradition, also outside ritual contexts *stricto sensu.* Brahmins in particular preferred self-imposed expiations to punishments imposed by
rulers. These self-imposed expiations could be extremely severe and
might even result in death. This does not change the fact that they
are not obviously compatible with karmic retribution. Indeed, certain Puranic passages suggest that expiations may be a way to avoid
karmic "punishment."

Having said this, it must be admitted that the notion of self-im-

posed restrictions so as to force karmic traces to mature is not necessarily in contradiction with karmic retribution. We saw that Jaina
asceticism was inspired by this idea: the self-imposed suffering of
the ascetics was believed to destroy traces of deeds carried out in the
past. The marriage between karmic retribution and Brahmanical expiation could therefore be solemnized, and the Brahmanical tradition did what it could to make this happen. The following passage—
from the *Devibhagavata Purana* (4.21.5–17)—illustrates this: "Men
must experience the karma that was formerly made, but can that not
be worn away by pilgrimage, asceticism, and gifts? For the rites of expiation have been set forth in the legal treatises composed by the noble sages in order to destroy the evils amassed in former lives." The
Brahmanical expiations are here on a par with asceticism (along with
pilgrimage and gifts). Both destroy traces of former deeds, presumably by forcing karma to "ripen."

CHAPTER 7

From One Life to the Next

The mental state at the precise moment of death is often considered to be particularly important for determining the nature of the next existence. In a certain sense this is not in conflict with the belief in karmic retribution, because the state one is in at the moment of death might be thought of as the end result of a whole life, and therefore as representative of what this life had been like. However, this is not always the case: one's final mental state may not be representative of the life it concludes, but rather may be exceptional and unforeseen. Emphasizing the mental state at the moment of death introduces in such cases an element that may be to some extent in contradiction with the general tenor of the life concerned. The role attributed to this mental state is therefore ambiguous: depending on the circumstances, it may extend and confirm the importance of karmic retribution, or it may be separate from it (and perhaps even in contradiction with it).

Jainism

In Jainism the moment of death is also, for some very advanced practitioners, the moment of liberation. It is a delicate moment, at which all karma has been exhausted and no new karma is created. The importance of this precise moment of liberation allows us to expect that the moment of death of less special individuals, too, will be particularly significant in Jainism, the more so since the Jainas consider the transition from one life to the next to be immediate.

This is indeed the case. The mental state just before death plays an important role in Jainism, and reincarnation is believed to take place immediately after death. This attitude with regard to the final mental state may take a negative form, as when a commentator claims that a man who dies in the act of sexual intercourse is reborn in the womb of his partner. The positive expression of the assumed importance of one's state at the moment of death is more important. It is behind an essential feature of Jaina religiosity: the desire to choose and control one's own death.

This holy, self-chosen death is called *sallekhana* in Jainism. The Jainas emphatically distinguish it from other forms of suicide, which they consider "impure," unlike *sallekhana,* which is "pure." *Sallekhana* is the conscious and conscientious abstention from all food, in a gradual manner that never disrupts the practitioner's inner peace or dispassionate mindfulness. Such a death will have a positive effect on one's next incarnation, yet it is important that *sallekhana* be untainted by any desires pertaining to rebirth, to the extension of the current life span, to a rapid death, or to the prospect of sensual pleasures in the future that were not attained in this life. In spite of the hardships connected with this form of holy death, it is certain that many Jainas over the centuries have chosen and carried out such a death.

The ideal of a chosen and pure death finds expression in a canonical text of the Jainas (*Uttaradhyanana* 5):

These two ways of life ending with death have been declared: death with one's will and death against one's will.

Death against one's will is that of ignorant men, and it happens to the same individual many times. Death with one's will is that of wise men, and at best it happens but once....

Full of peace and without injury to any one is, as I have heard from my teachers, the death of the virtuous who control themselves and subdue their senses....

When under discipline he lives piously even as a householder, he will, on quitting flesh and bones, share the world of the gods called Yakshas.

Now a restrained monk will become one of the two: either one free from all misery or a god of great power....

Having heard this from the venerable men who control themselves and subdue their senses, the virtuous and the learned do not tremble in the hour of death....

When the right time to prepare for death has arrived, a faithful monk should in the presence of his teacher suppress all emotions of fear and joy and wait for the dissolution of his body.

When the time for quitting the body has come, a sage dies the death with one's will.

Buddhism

In Buddhism the emphasis on the moment of death is less pronounced, yet present here and there. A canonical Buddhist text introduces the notion, be it in a somewhat secondary position (*Majjhima Nikaya* III, pp. 214–215: *Mahakammavibhanga Sutta*):

As to the person here who kills living beings, takes what is not given, misconducts himself in sensual pleasures, speaks falsehood, speaks maliciously, speaks harshly, gossips, is covetous, has a mind of ill will, and holds wrong view, and on the dissolution of the body, after death, he reappears in a happy destination, even in the heavenly world: either earlier he did a good action to be felt as pleasant, or later he did a good action to be felt as pleasant, *or at the time of death he acquired and undertook right view....*

As to the person here who abstains from killing living beings, from taking what is not given, from misconduct in sensual pleasures, from false speech, from malicious speech, from harsh speech, from gossip, is not covetous, his mind is without ill will, and holds right view, and on the dissolution of the body, after death, he reappears in a state of deprivation, in an unhappy destination, in perdition, even in hell: either earlier he did an evil action to be felt as painful, or later he did an evil action to be felt as painful, *or at the time of death he acquired and undertook wrong view.*

The belief in the importance of one's final volition just before death still appears to be accepted as determining the nature of the immediately following rebirth in a number of Buddhist countries. The *Visuddhimagga* (Path of Purification), a manual of Theravada Buddhism, describes in its seventeenth chapter in some detail what final thoughts lead to what rebirths.

According to certain Buddhists, an intermediary being fills the gap between death and the reincarnation into a next body. This intermediary being is sometimes called *gandharva* and exists for the unspecified period of time that elapses between two succeeding incarnations until it finds an appropriate next body in which to incarnate. An important Buddhist scholastic work, the *Abhidharmakosha Bhashya* of Vasubandhu (commenting on verse 3.15), describes the final part of the process as follows:

> An intermediate being is produced with a view to going to the place of its realm of rebirth where it should go. It possesses, by virtue of its actions, the divine eye. Even though distant he sees the place of his rebirth. There he sees his father and mother united. His mind is troubled by the effects of sex and hostility. When the intermediate being is male, it is gripped by a male desire with regard to the mother; when it is female, it is gripped by a female desire with regard to the father.

At first sight this passage brings to mind the Freudian Oedipus complex, but strictly speaking it says nothing of the kind (it is not the child but the intermediary being that feels passion for one of the parents). It states that the final state of mind of the intermediary being determines where and in what state a person will be reborn. This is not quite the same as claiming that the mental state at the moment of death is decisive, but shares some features with it. The mental state just before the moment of reincarnation determines in both these cases where exactly this reincarnation is going to take place. This moment just before reincarnation, in the Buddhist scholastic case, is no longer the moment just before death, but the final moment of the intermediary being.

The notion of a *gandharva* who plays a role in reincarnation is already known to Buddhist canonical literature. One passage (*Majjhima Nikaya* I, pp. 265–266) presents it as follows:

> Monks, the conception of an embryo in a womb takes place through the union of three things. Here, there is the union of the

mother and father, but it is not the mother's season, and the *gan-dharva* is not present—in this case there is no conception of an embryo in a womb. Here, there is the union of the mother and father, and it is the mother's season, but the *gandharva* is not present—in this case, too, there is no conception of an embryo in a womb. But when there is the union of the mother and the father, and it is the mother's season, and the *gandharva* is present, through the union of these three things the conception of an embryo in a womb takes place.

It is most likely that Vasubandhu based his idea of an intermediary being on a passage like this. However, not all Buddhists interpreted the passage in this manner. Theravada Buddhism—the form of Buddhism that survives in Sri Lanka, Thailand, and some other countries of Southeast Asia—did not think that this passage obliged them to abandon the notion that rebirth takes place instantaneously, without the help of any intermediary being. The *gandharva* mentioned in this passage is, according to them, the being about to enter into the womb, right from a previous life.

The Brahmanical Tradition

The Brahmanical tradition did not originally know and accept the doctrine of rebirth and karmic retribution. It came to adopt this belief, but not without retaining some of its own earlier conceptions. The result was a mixture of ideas that do not always fit well together.

Let us first consider a passage from the *Brihadaranyaka Upanishad* (4.4.3–4), which may be among the first Brahmanical passages to describe the transition from one life to the next:

It is like this. As a caterpillar, when it comes to the tip of a blade of grass, reaches out to a new foothold and draws itself onto it, so the self, after it has knocked down this body and rendered it unconscious, reaches out to a new foothold and draws itself onto it.

It is like this. As a weaver, after she has removed the colored yarn, weaves a different design that is newer and more attractive, so the self, after it has knocked down this body and rendered it unconscious, makes for himself a different figure that is newer and more attractive—the figure of a forefather, or of a Gandharva, or of a god, or of Prajapati, or of Brahma, or else the figure of some other being.

The latter half of this passage is interesting in that it reveals that the early Brahmins who adopted the belief in rebirth and karmic retribution (or at any rate some of them) interpreted this belief in a very positive manner: the self creates for itself a better existence, among the gods and other supernatural beings, not, it appears, among humans. This, as we know, is only half of the belief as it was generally accepted, and this one-sided version of it could not survive for long in the Brahmanical tradition.

We have already had occasion to mention the Brahmanical *shraddha,* the ritual of feeding dead ancestors. This ritual seems to presuppose a different fate after death from that of rebirth determined by one's acts, and originally it no doubt did. However, the rite survived into the time when rebirth and karmic retribution had become generally accepted. This in its turn led to new ideas about what happens after death. The disembodied spirits of deceased ancestors (known as *pretas*) now came to be thought of as intermediary beings, bridging the period following one's death and preceding one's next incarnation. Further refinements were sometimes introduced, resulting in a succession of intermediary beings, but these details are of less interest to us at present.

What is of interest to us is that the Brahmanical tradition is not unanimous in this regard. The following passage from the *Mahabharata* (3.181.23–24), which is put in the mouth of sage Markandeya and addresses Kaunteya, illustrates this: "Man in his original, God-created body piles up a great lot of good and bad acts. At the end of his life he abandons his mostly deteriorated carcass and is *instantly* reborn in a womb; *there is no intermediary being.*" The term here used for "intermediary being"—*antarabhava*—is also the one used in the Buddhist *Abhidharmakosha Bhashya* (considered above) and elsewhere. The explicit denial of the existence of such a being in this passage shows that the notion was familiar to its author, but that he rejected it.

The notion that one's mental state at the moment of death determines one's next birth is not unknown to Brahmanism either.

The *Padma Purana* (2.1.5.1–35) tells the amusing story of a virtuous man who, being frightened by demons at the moment of his death, thought, "Demons!" and was therefore reborn as a demon. The *Garuda Purana* (*Uttara Khanda* 22.17) gives a curious twist to this notion by attributing great importance to the mental state of the father at the moment of impregnation: "Whatever a man has on his mind at the time of impregnation, a creature born of such a nature will enter the womb." In modern Hinduism sacred formulas may be recited into the right ear of a dying person.

CHAPTER 8

Devotion

Our discussion of the way philosophers found a place for God to account for karmic retribution has confronted us with the question of whether their God was really barely more than a karmic accountant, someone who strictly followed the rules of karmic retribution, rules that He had neither invented nor ordained. In one way the answer must be yes, for there was not much else for God to do in their depiction of the world. We may, however, suspect that these thinkers attributed more importance than that of a mere intellectual stopgap to God. And if they didn't, others did. Some were of the opinion that the concept of God as the servant of karmic retribution was topsy-turvy: God did not recompense acts because the law of karma told him to, but rather it was the other way round: the law of karma was effective because God wanted it that way.

An interesting illustration of this point of view finds expression in a passage that the fourteenth-century author Sayana Madhava ascribes to the Pashupatas, philosophers who were also worshipers of the God Shiva:

> In other systems the cause of things acts in dependence upon something else [i.e., karma]; but here God is independent....
>
> But an opponent might say: This is a major delusion to think that the independent Lord is the cause, for if He were, two faults would appear: deeds would produce no result and all effects would be produced at the same time.
>
> [To this the Pashupatas may answer:] You should suppose no such thing, because each factor has its place.

[Opponent:] But if the independent Lord were the cause, deeds would be fruitless.

[Pashupata:] Suppose they were, what then?

[Opponent:] Then there would be no motive for action.

[Pashupata:] We ask, to whom do you ascribe this absence of motive that causes deeds to be fruitless? To the doer or to the Lord? Not to the first, because the deed is fruitful when it is favored by the will of God and can never bear fruit when it is not favored by the Lord... But this much is not sufficient to prevent us from work, for we see how the husbandman works, and men act because they are dependent upon the will of God. Nor to the second, for the Lord, inasmuch as all his desires are already satisfied, does not depend upon any motive furnished by karma.

In regard to the objection that all effects would be produced at the same time, this also does not hold. Because we must admit that the power of unobstructed action by which the Lord, who is of inconceivable power, causes all effects, is a power that follows his will.

The upshot of this passage is that only deeds that are favored by God bear fruit, not deeds that are not favored by God. The passage still tries to convince us that God's independence should not discourage us from acting, just as the fact that God is the cause of his harvest does not stop a husbandman from plowing his fields. In other words, God is not bound by the rules of karma yet favors them in normal circumstances.

This passage remains relatively theoretical. A far more personal attitude toward the highest God became predominant in a development in the Indian religions that centered on devotion *(bhakti).*

Devotion of believers to a god they worship is a regular feature of religion, both in and outside India. The specific form of devotion that in the course of time came to play an all-important role in the religions of India and that we call *bhakti* differs from ordinary forms of devotion in that it is an instrument to reach the highest goal. *Bhakti* competes with other methods to reach this religious goal and to some extent even affects the nature of the goal: it may no longer be thought of as liberation from rebirth, but as proximity to the highest God.

In principle there can be devotion with regard to any highest God; in reality the most noticeable forms of *bhakti* occur in connection with the Gods Shiva and Vishnu, and specifically with two incarnations of the latter: Krishna and Rama.

The *Bhagavadgita* is one of the early texts in which devotion to Krishna is presented as a religious goal, or rather as a means to arrive at disinterested action, itself a means to the highest goal. Devotion to God is also presented as a means in the *Yoga Sutra,* this time as a means to reach yogic meditation. The *bhakti* of these and other early texts has none of the intensity and emotion that characterized *bhakti* in some of its more recent manifestations.

Bhakti of the more emotional kind may have begun in the south of the subcontinent (even though some scholars do not accept this view). Its earliest surviving expressions (ca. sixth to tenth centuries C.E.) are Tamil compositions by the poets called the Alvars (who were worshipers of Vishnu) and the Nayanars (worshipers of Shiva). The fact that a number of these poets were not Brahmins, combined with the fact that this literature as well as the Brahmanical literature that adopted this kind of *bhakti* is critical of the Brahmanical social order, supports the thesis that emotional *bhakti* was and remained for some time an expression of non-Brahmanical religiosity.

The *Bhagavata Purana* was composed in the south, probably during the last two centuries of the first millennium C.E., and gives expression to the emotional *bhakti* of the Alvars but now in Sanskrit. It testifies to the absorption of this feature into the Brahmanical tradition, while yet emphasizing that *bhakti* is superior to everything else, including Vedic study and Vedic rites.

Bhakti subsequently found expression in numerous works by many authors, an important number of whom remained critical with regard to the Brahmanical social system with its division into caste classes. Even those who did not object to this system agreed that *bhakti* as a religious practice was open to men and women (!) of all layers of society.

For the devotees, devotion to the supreme God is a, or even the, way to free oneself from the burden of karma, at least according to certain texts. This conviction becomes stronger over time, and devotional religion succeeds in gaining an all-important position on the Indian religious scene.

Devotion to God is, of course, only possible if there is a supreme God one believes in. The currents that we have mainly considered so far—Buddhism, Jainism, part of the Brahmanical tradition—had no place for such a supreme God. Indeed, the acceptance of rebirth and karmic retribution is not always easy to reconcile with such a belief. Even those (most specifically thinkers of the Nyaya and Vaisheshika schools) who introduced the notion of a supreme God in order to render karmic retribution intelligible, accepted a God who was a bookkeeper rather than a supreme ruler. If their God were to interfere with karmic retribution, the very justification and need to believe in Him would disappear.

However, there were people in India who believed in a supreme and omnipotent God, and their numbers became ever more important. These people had to rethink some issues, for their God was not tied hands and feet by the rules of karma. Quite on the contrary, their God was supposed to be above these rules and independent of them.

A comparison of the relative powers of various causal factors in the life of human beings is found in the *Shvetashvatara Upanishad* (1.1–3):

> People who make inquiries about the highest principle say:
> What is the cause of the highest principle? Why were we born? By what do we live? On what are we established? Governed by whom do we live in pleasure and in pain, each in our respective situation?
> Should we regard it as time, as inherent nature, as necessity, as chance, as the elements, as the source of birth, or as the Person? Or is it a combination of these? But that can't be, because there is the self. Even the self is not in control, because it is itself subject to pleasure and pain.
> Those who follow the discipline of meditation have seen the power of God and of the self, all hidden by their own qualities. One alone is he who governs all those causes, from "time" to "self."

The passage is ambiguous in the original Sanskrit, and it is therefore not clear whether this translation correctly expresses the intention of its author. There can, however, be no doubt that it enumerates a number of causal factors and subordinates them all to one higher entity, God. Interestingly, karma does not figure in this list, but necessity *(niyati)* does. This term for necessity is also the one used in Ajivikism, and the strict determinism of this religion was at bottom of a karmic nature. We may assume that the *Shvetashvatara Upanishad* subordinates karma, too, to the power of God.

The *Mahabharata* speaks regularly of a creator God, whom it calls "Arranger." About this Arranger, it says (12.224.50): "Some people, experts of karma, call him 'human effort'. Other wise men, who reflect upon the nature of living beings, call him 'fate.'" In other words, God the Arranger is behind karma and fate, and transcends them.

The *Bhagavadgita* is one of the early texts that preach devotion to God. God here has taken the human form of Krishna, and it is Krishna who dispenses the teachings contained in this text. Addressing himself to the warrior Arjuna, son of Pandu, at one point he reveals his true form to him. Having taken on his human form again, Krishna then says (11.53–55):

> Not by the Vedas nor by austerity, nor by gifts or acts of worship, can I be seen in such a guise, as thou hast seen Me.
>
> But by unswerving devotion can I in such a guise, Arjuna, be known and seen in very truth, and entered into, scorcher of the foe.
>
> Doing My work, intent on Me, devoted to Me, free from attachment, free from enmity to all beings, who is so, goes to Me, son of Pandu.

We see that the highest aim that devotion can lead to is *going to God,* whatever that precisely means. The emphasis shifts from liberation as highest aim to being with God. This can be illustrated by comparing the following two verses of the same text, *Bhagavadgita* 2.72 and 8.5. The former of these two verses speaks about a specific yogic state and says the following about it: "He who abides therein also at the moment of death, he reaches the *brahmanirvana.*" It may not be fully clear what is meant by *brahmanirvana,* but it is beyond doubt that it is a way to designate liberation.

The next of these two verses (8.5) does not speak of yoga, but of devotion to God: "He who dies remembering only me at the moment of death, when abandoning his body, he will go to my state of being; there is not doubt about this." Both these verses emphasize the importance of one's mental state at the moment of death. But where the first one promises liberation to a person who has done the necessary, the second one speaks of reaching the state of being of God. This shift of emphasis—perhaps one should say change of goal—is typical for devotional religion in South Asia. Belief in rebirth and karmic retribution is not abandoned, even though this process is no longer thought of as impersonal and independent of God's will. Indeed, the whole karmic burden, including the social class to which one belongs, can be bypassed by devotion to God (9.32): "Those who come to me for refuge—even if they are born in sin or are women, Vaishyas, or Shudras—they will reach the highest goal."

Loss of interest in liberation becomes prominent in devotional literature. Later devotional texts may even say so in so many words, as does Rupagoswami's *Bhaktirasamritasindhu:* "Those devotees who have found rest for their mind in the service of Krishna's lotus-feet will never desire liberation." Some even claim that devotion is a higher state than liberation. Other devotional authors, especially those who proclaim emotional forms of devotion, present a complicated image of karma. For them, God (usually in the form of Krishna) removes karma if he so wishes, but these same deeds are an obstacle to the religious endeavors of the devotee—that is, to his attempts to get close to God by means of devotion.

Concluding Comments

DEVELOPMENTS OUTSIDE THE INDIAN SUBCONTINENT

Belief in reincarnation was known in ancient Greece. Herodotus claimed that this belief originally came from Egypt, but in this he was no doubt mistaken. The belief is frequently ascribed to Pythagoras, while the Orphic traditions, too, were associated with it. Plato argues for the prior existence and immortality of the soul, and may have believed in reincarnation. The later Pythagorean tradition maintained that Pythagoras had been a recipient of Indian wisdom, but this may be a more recent invention. Pythagoras lived in the sixth century B.C.E., well before the Buddha and Mahavira (who appear to have lived in the fifth century B.C.E.), and presumably even longer before the belief in rebirth and karmic retribution spread in India beyond its homeland in Greater Magadha.

Indian notions of rebirth and karmic retribution did travel westward, and the religion called Manichaeism was certainly one of its principal means of transport. The founder of this religion, Mani (third century C.E.), is known to have spent time in northwest India, and his religion contains elements that he borrowed from Buddhism. It may be through Manichaeism that these notions found their way into some forms of Jewish Kabbala, Christian Gnosticism (including the more recent Cathars), and Shiite Islam.

The most important manner in which the notion of rebirth and karmic retribution traveled beyond its Indian homeland was as part of the religious spread of Brahmanism and Buddhism. Brahmanism traveled to Southeast Asia in particular, and even though Brahmanism should here primarily be thought of as a sociopolitical ideology, it was normally accompanied by religious elements, such as the worship of Shiva or Vishnu. Rebirth and karmic retribution were often part of the package of beliefs and ideas that settled in those faraway lands. In the case of Buddhism, its link with rebirth and karmic retribution was even closer, and this belief presented itself wherever Buddhism gained a foothold.

However, belief in rebirth and karmic retribution was a so far un-known element in many of the countries where Brahmanism and Buddhism were introduced, and some regions were less prepared than others to adopt it. An example is Bali, where we find an inter-esting mixture of religions in which Brahmanical and Buddhist ele-ments are prominently present, but which is yet devoid of the belief in karmic retribution. Others do not reject the belief but tend to in-terpret it metaphorically. This is particularly true of certain authors from modern Buddhist countries, including Sri Lanka and Japan.

WHAT DOES IT ALL MEAN?

In a general way one could say that the belief in rebirth and karmic retribution presupposes that morality is part of the structure of the universe. All those who accept this belief in one form or another are convinced that good deeds will be rewarded and bad deeds punished. This conviction did not need a god, even though the supervision of karmic retribution came to be attributed to an accountant God by some in the Brahmanical tradition. The acceptance of a supreme God sometimes had the opposite effect: rather than explaining and strengthening the process of karmic retribution, God might provide shortcuts, preferably to those who were devoted to Him.

The moral side of karmic retribution deserves some further re-flection. The morality that accompanied this belief was not always the same. Perhaps unsurprisingly, ascetically oriented religious movements—most notably Jainism and Buddhism—considered deeds "good" if they were as close as possible to the ascetic life-style. Numerous abstentions—from stealing, from sexuality, and from much else—were believed to lead to agreeable results in future lives, and lack of restraint almost guaranteed a disagreeable outcome. The Brahmanical tradition, as so often, was less uniform in its ideas about morality. Those most taken in by ascetical ideals had rather similar notions as the Jainas and the Buddhists about what is good and what is not. Most Brahmins, however, linked the belief in karmic retribution to their vision of what constitutes the correct order of so-ciety. The Brahmanical vision of society gave all individuals a fixed place and expected from them that they would behave accordingly. In this vision, the best anyone could do was to act in accordance with his or her position in life, and this, inevitably, was presented in Brahmanical circles as the most reliable or even only way to obtain a good rebirth.

It follows from these reflections that our initial observation to the extent that the belief in karmic retribution implies a moral order that governs the universe, though correct, is in need of specification. Everyone agreed that good deeds lead to good results, but not everyone agreed in all cases on what is a good deed. Various beliefs about the ideal form of life, or of society, have to be taken into consideration, and the resulting differences can be striking. The warrior Arjuna was told in the *Bhagavadgita* that waging war against his kinsmen was "a good thing," something that would have good results; this was the, or a, Brahmanical view. Contemporary Buddhists might not agree, and might look upon this same Arjuna as no better than a murderer, whose chances of a decent rebirth were severely jeopardized by his warlike behavior. In other words, belief in karmic retribution implies a moral order, but which moral order? The answer to this question will depend on whom you ask, and in the Indian situation there were representatives of many different points of view ready to give different answers.

There is another possible way of looking at the belief in rebirth and karmic retribution, not so much as an expression of a fundamental concern with questions of morality, but rather as a way to make sense of certain forms of human behavior. In order to understand this, it will be necessary to recall some of the observations made at the beginning of this book. We saw that the belief in rebirth and karmic retribution was thought of in early India as giving rise to a problem. The religious currents and practices we considered did not look forward to rebirth and rather developed methods to put an end to it. One of these methods is immobilization asceticism, another the realization that one's inner self never acts and remains therefore untouched by karmic retribution. These solutions, we had occasion to point out, fit the problem like a glove, or rather like two gloves.

Exactly the same two "gloves" existed in early Christianity but were not there looked upon as solutions that would free a person from rebirth and karmic retribution. Let me explain.

At the time of the Roman empire, when persecutions of Christians came to an end, a number of Christians turned to voluntary asceticism. Numerous accounts have survived of the ascetic practices to which these Christians subjected themselves, and they share a common theme: a central element of these practices was immobilization. There is no need to recall the feats of the pillar saints or of all those others who faced great bodily torment in positions that remained as immobile as possible. We saw already that these forms of asceticism can be looked upon as the continuation of earlier persecutions that at least some Christians had sought with much gusto and that, like the later forms of asceticism but with inevitable differences, consisted in facing bodily torment without yielding to pressure.

However, there were other early Christians who believed in the inactive nature of the human self. These Christians are often referred to as Gnostics, and they believed that the inner core of human beings is a spark of God. God, moreover, they thought of as completely inactive. The knowledge of one's deepest inner nature as being a spark of God, and therefore inactive, was a vital part of the belief of these Christians.

In early Christianity, the practice of immobilization and the belief in the unchangeable nature of one's inner self belonged to different subgroups. Christian ascetics and Christian Gnostics did not like each other and followed altogether different paths. And yet, both seem to share the hidden conviction that what they really are is different from their body. This allows the ascetic to abandon his body in sometimes spectacular ways and the Gnostic to hold on to his specific belief.

We are, then, confronted with the following remarkable situation. Both in ancient India and in early Christianity we find the same—or at any rate a closely similar—combination of practices and beliefs: the practice of ascetic immobilization and the belief in the inactive nature of one's inner self. In both cases those who perform the practice and those who hold the belief can be different individuals (and in the case of early Christianity they decidedly are). There is yet one major difference. In India this practice and this belief have their place in a more encompassing scheme of things: the scheme of rebirth and karmic retribution. This scheme goes a long way to explain why ascetics practiced in this particular manner and why this particular belief was popular. Early Christianity had no such scheme. The practice and the belief present themselves here as historical coincidences, with no clear and necessary link between them.

We have noted already that this practice and this belief, wherever they occur, give the impression that there is a hidden conviction that can be approximately formulated in the statement that one is different from one's body. The assumption that there is such a hidden conviction—unknown perhaps to the people involved—turns out to be very useful in understanding a number of different practices and beliefs, found in all continents and ranging from the belief in a free soul that plays no role in a person's activities to painful initiation practices. They all strengthen the impression that such a hidden conviction may be the result of a predisposition that could be innate.

If we now return to the scheme of rebirth and karmic retribution in India, our reflections suggest that we may in the end be mistaken in explaining immobilization asceticism and the belief in an inactive self as results of that scheme. It is equally possible and perhaps more likely that it is the other way round: this scheme is the result of an attempt at interpretation of the possibly inborn predisposition to practice immobilization asceticism and believe in an inactive self. If so, we may have to conclude that the study of rebirth and karmic retribution in India does not only tell us something about Indian culture, but perhaps something about our human nature as well.

Further Reading

For a discussion of the difficulties connected with translation, an issue touched upon in the Preface, see *The Translator's Invisibility: A History of Translation* by Lawrence Venuti (second edition, New York: Routledge, 2008). The warning against modern speculative opinions about karma comes from Peter Gaeffke, "Karma in North Indian Bhakti Traditions," *Journal of the American Oriental Society* 105:2 (1985), p. 273.

The belief in rebirth and karmic retribution covers many aspects of Indian religious and philosophical thought. This has the consequence that there are numerous publications about this or that specific aspect of this belief, but few about the phenomenon in general. One of the rare exceptions is *The Doctrine of Karma: Its Origin and Development in Brahmanical, Buddhist and Jaina Traditions* by Yuvraj Krishan (Delhi: Motilal Banarsidass, 1997), a book rich in information to be read with a critical eye.

The origin of the belief in rebirth and karmic retribution and its relationship with Vedic religion has been much debated. By and large, there are two opposing camps: either this belief arose in and out of Vedic religion, or it originated elsewhere and subsequently affected Vedic religion. I have argued for the second position in my book *Greater Magadha: Studies in the Culture of Early India* (Leiden: Brill, 2007), and this is the position I have presented in the early chapters of the present book. Representative of the first position is, for example, *The Vedic Origins of Karma: Cosmos as Man in Ancient Indian Myth and Ritual* by Herman W. Tull (State University of New York Press, 1989). The special position of Buddhism, also with respect to the special twist it gave to the belief in rebirth and karmic retribution, is explained in my *Buddhist Teaching in India* (Boston: Wisdom, 2009). The consequences of a close reading of the oft-repeated canonical passage presenting the path of the Buddha are explored in my *Absorption: Two Studies of Human Nature* (part 2; http://www .bronkhorst-absorption.info/).

The role played by karma in religious life is a topic that receives attention in a volume called *Karma and Rebirth in Classical Indian Traditions* edited by Wendy Doniger O'Flaherty (University of California Press, 1980). This volume contains a dozen contributions by different scholars dealing with karma and rebirth in Hinduism, Buddhism, and Jainism. Similar, but concentrating on more recent developments inside and outside the Indian subcontinent, is *Karma and Rebirth: Post Classical Developments,* edited by Ronald W. Neufeldt (State University of New York Press, 1983), with contributions by eighteen different authors.

An overview of the ways in which Indian philosophers dealt with the belief can be found in *Karma und Wiedergeburt im indischen Denken* by Wilhelm Halbfass (Kreuzlingen-Munich: Hugendubel, 2000). This work has not been translated into English, and unfortunately no book in English of comparable scope is known to me. The extensive elaborations that the karma doctrine underwent in Jainism in particular receive attention in most scholarly presentations of this religion, such as *The Jaina Path of Purification* by Padmanabh S. Jaini (Delhi: Motilal Banarsidass, 1979, esp. pp. 111–133), *The Jains* by Paul Dundas (second edition, London and New York: Routledge, 2002, esp. pp. 97–105), and *The Doctrine of the Jainas, Described after the Old Sources* by Walther Schubring (Delhi: Motilal Banarsidass, 2000, esp. pp. 172-195); see further *Harmless Souls: Karmic Bondage and Religious Change in Early Jainism with Special Reference to Umasvati and Kundakunda* by W. J. Johnson (Delhi: Motilal Banarsidass, 1995). The struggles of Indian philosophers to make sense of the undeniable teleological elements that are associated with karmic retribution have been presented and analyzed in my *Karma and Teleology: A Problem and Its Solutions in Indian Philosophy* (Tokyo: The International Institute for Buddhist Studies, 2000). For Ajivikism, *History and Doctrines of the Ajivikas: A Vanished Indian Religion* by A. L. Basham (reprint, Delhi: Motilal Banarsidass, 1981) remains a classic, even though further progress has meanwhile been made regarding the role of karma in this religion.

For overviews of the issue of "transfer of merit," two authors in particular should be mentioned: Minoru Hara ("Transfer of Merit in Hindu Literature and Religion," *The Memoirs of the Toyo Bunko* 52

[1994], pp. 103–135) and Albrecht Wezler ("On the Gaining of Merit and the Incurring of Demerit through the Agency of Others, I: Deeds by Proxy," *Lex et Litterae: Studies in Honour of Oscar Botto,* edited by Siegfried Lienhard and Irma Piovano [Alessandria (Italy): Edizioni dell'Orso, 1997, pp. 567–589]; at the end of this article there is a long "List of Works and Articles on 'Transfer of Merit'"). The uneasy relationship between karma and curses receives attention in two articles by William L. Smith: "Explaining the Inexplicable: Uses of the Curse in Rama Literature," *Kalyanamitraraganam: Essays in Honour of Nils Simonsson,* edited by Eivind Kahrs (Oxford University Press, 1986, pp. 261–276) and "Changing Bodies: The Mechanics of the Metamorphic Curse," *Acta Orientalia* 56 (1995), pp. 125–143. For a study of Time as fate, see Yaroslav Vassilkov, "Kalavada (the Doctrine of Cyclical Time) in the *Mahabharata* and the Concept of Heroic Didactics," in *Composing a Tradition: Concepts, Techniques and Relationships, Proceedings of the First Dubrovnik International Conference on the Sanskrit Epics and Puranas,* edited by Mary Brockington and Peter Schreiner (Zagreb: Croatian Academy of Sciences and Arts 1999, pp. 17–33).

The concluding reflections draw upon my article "Asceticism, Religion and Biological Evolution," *Method and Theory in the Study of Religion* 13 (2001), pp. 374–418.

Beside the publications already mentioned, the following provide additional information with regard to the background knowledge presented:

Oskar von Hinüber's *A Handbook of Pali Literature* (Berlin and New York: Walter de Gruyter, 1996) is the most complete and reliable overview of Buddhist canonical literature in Pali to date. This same author ("The Foundation of the Bhikkhunisamgha: A Contribution to the Earliest History of Buddhism," *Annual Report of the International Research Institute for Advanced Buddhology at Soka University for the Academic Year 2007* [2008], 3–35) has presented arguments for the claim that there were no nuns during the lifetime of the Buddha. Hajime Nakamura's *Indian Buddhism: A Survey with Bibliographical Notes* (Japan: KUFS Publication, 1980) is still useful and covers also Buddhist canonical texts preserved in other languages. For Vedic literature, Jan Gonda's *Vedic Literature* (Wiesbaden: Otto Harrassowitz, 1975) remains the standard reference work.

Sheldon Pollock's *The Language of the Gods in the World of Men* (University of California Press, 2006) contains lots of information relevant to the transformation and spread of Brahmanism, even though Pollock does not interpret these data in these terms.

The question of "Class, Species and Universal in Indian Philosophy" has been explored and documented in *"Caste" et philosophie bouddhique* by Vincent Eltschinger (Vienna: Vienna University, 2000). Information about the early history of Indian philosophy can be found in my *Aux origines de la philosophie indienne* (Gollion, 2008). A full investigation into the ways in which different philosophical schools dealt with one shared issue in particular, the problems associated with propositions like "the potter makes a pot," is provided in my *Language and Reality: On an Episode in Indian Thought* (Leiden: Brill, 2011).

The chapter called "Bhakti" by David N. Lorenzen in *The Hindu World* (ed. S. Mittal and G. Thursby; New York and London: Routledge, 2004) provides a useful and accessible overview of this phenomenon. On the South Indian origin of emotional *bhakti*, Friedhelm Hardy's *Viraha-Bhakti: The Early History of Krsna Devotion in South India* (Oxford University Press, 1983) remains valuable.

Note finally that most of the translations of upanishadic passages have been taken from Patrick Olivelle's *The Early Upanisads* (Oxford University Press, 1998), passages of the *Laws of Manu* from his *Manu's Code of Law* (Oxford University Press, 2005), and passages of the *Mahabharata* (to the extent available) from J. A. B. van Buitenen's *The Mahabharata*, 3 vols. (University of Chicago Press, 1973–1978). Translations of passages from the Buddhist canon often come from Maurice Walshe's *The Long Discourses of the Buddha,* from Bhikkhu Nanamoli and Bhikkhu Bodhi's *The Middle Length Discourses of the Buddha,* and from Bhikkhu Bodhi's *The Connected Discourses of the Buddha* (Boston: Wisdom Publications, 1987, 1995, and 2000). For Vasubandhu's *Abhidharmakosha Bhashya* I have used Leo M. Pruden's *Abhidharmakosabhasyam by Louis de La Vallée Poussin,* English translation (Berkeley: Asian Humanities Press, 1988–1990). Translations have been modified slightly for consistency of punctuation.

Index

About the Author

Johannes Bronkhorst is professor of Sanskrit and Indian studies at the University of Lausanne (Switzerland), where he has taught since 1987. He studied Indian literature in India, mainly at the University of Pune, but obtained a second doctorate at the University of Leiden (Netherlands) in 1980. He has published widely in the field of Sanskrit literature and Indian thought, including the study of Brahmanism, Buddhism, and Jainism.